# PERGAMON INSTITUTE OF ENGLISH (OXFORD)

*Materials for Language Practice*

D1795535

**Other Titles in this Series Include:**

BINHAM, Philip *et al*
*Hotel English**
Communicating with the International Traveller

CRANE, Anthony
*Marketing English**

FITZPATRICK, Antony
*English for International Conferences**

McKELLEN, Joy and Mavis Spooner
*Business Matters**
A guide to commercial correspondence in English

ZINKIN, Taya
*Write Right*
A guide to effective communication in English

* Includes audio cassettes

# RESTAURANT ENGLISH

## COMMUNICATING WITH THE INTERNATIONAL TRAVELLER

Philip Binham, Riitta Lampola, James Murray

PERGAMON PRESS

OXFORD · NEW YORK · TORONTO
SYDNEY · PARIS · FRANKFURT

| U.K. | Pergamon Press Ltd., Headington Hill Hall, Oxford OX3 0BW, England |
| U.S.A. | Pergamon Press Inc., Maxwell House, Fairview Park, Elmsford, New York 10523, U.S.A. |
| CANADA | Pergamon Press Canada Ltd., Suite 104, 150 Consumers Road, Willowdale, Ontario M2J 1P9, Canada |
| AUSTRALIA | Pergamon Press (Aust.) Pty. Ltd., P.O. Box 544, Potts Point, N.S.W. 2011, Australia |
| FRANCE | Pergamon Press SARL, 24 rue des Ecoles, 75240 Paris, Cedex 05, France |
| FEDERAL REPUBLIC OF GERMANY | Pergamon Press GmbH, 6242 Kronberg-Taunus, Hammerweg 6, Federal Republic of Germany |

First edition 1982

**British Library Cataloguing in Publication Data**
Binham, Philip
Restaurant English. - (Pergamon Institute of
English (Oxford) materials for language practice)
1. English language - Text-books for foreigners
2. English language - Conversation and phrase
books
I. Title   II. Lampola, Riitta
III. Murray, James
428.3′4     PE1128
ISBN 0-08-025339-3

**Library of Congress Catalog Card no: 81-81255**

*Printed in Great Britain by A. Wheaton & Co. Ltd., Exeter*

# CONTENTS

*Contents*

# INTRODUCTION

THIS material is designed for restaurant personnel in work or training who deal with English-speaking guests of different nationalities and who already have a knowledge of English but need to familiarize themselves with the language and phraseology of the profession. More specifically it is for those who need to understand customers' questions and statements, to reply to them appropriately, to supply information from tabulated data and to produce statements and questions of their own.

The chapters are presented situationally and consist of authentic dialogues and information for reference and exploitation, offering maximum exposure to context rather than rigid sets of artificial language exercises. It is for this reason that the recorded material is so vital. Restaurants in England and Finland have been chosen to provide a fairly flexible international setting.

*Cassette One* presents the principal dialogues and phrases of each chapter for listening and reproduction. These are marked in the book with the symbol ⌷⌷ . Space is not included on the tape for repetition.

*Cassette Two* consists of exercises which require manipulation of the items presented in the book and should be attempted once each chapter has been fully studied. The type of exercise varies according to the situation, having been chosen for usefulness or proximity to reality and not for structural features. In some cases guidelines are provided for correct production and in others the ability to interpret and respond to statements and questions covered in the chapter is tested. None of the exercises is self-correcting but a standard length of space is included in the recordings for the answers. Many of them are quite difficult and students will have to listen several times and make notes before attempting their replies.

The dialogues, phrases and exercises have been recorded at almost normal speed and with a variety of accents to accustom learners to the sort of language they have to encounter in their jobs.

The material can be used by students working on their own but is best utilised with a selective and resourceful teacher who can monitor performance and organise pair and group work.

N.B.   The material conforms to etiquette usually practised in the UK and Europe. Not much attention is given to the description of dishes and the language of cooking since this varies so much from region to region and is more relevant to chefs than to waiters or restaurant managers. Students may, however, usefully refer to the list of specialities in the last two chapters.

# Chapter 1
# RUNNING THE BUSINESS

## Types of restaurant

**CAFE/ CAFETERIA**  Small restaurants mainly concentrating on cakes, sandwiches, coffee and tea. Choice of food often very limited. No alcoholic beverages.

**SNACK BAR**  Modest restaurants where customers collect their food on trays at counters and carry it to the tables. Choice of dishes is based on convenience and speed, with foods like hamburgers, sausages and sandwiches.

**PUB**  Originally a British public house licensed to serve beer and other alcoholic beverages. Customers get their drinks from the counter and either stand there or sit at the tables. Some light snacks like pies and sandwiches are served; nowadays you can also have more substantial meals at many pubs.

**FISH AND CHIP SHOP**  A very British institution, where you can buy chips and deep-fried fish, usually cod, wrapped in paper to take away.

**INN/TAVERN**  Moderately-priced small restaurants which are often run by a private family in the countryside. The atmosphere is often very friendly and the food can be delicious.

**TERRACE RESTAURANT**  Situated out-of-doors and usually connected with a hotel or a restaurant. Open during the summertime only.

1

| | |
|---|---|
| *CANTEEN* | Usually connected with a school, office or factory. A place where students or workers have their lunch and coffee breaks. |
| *HAMBURGER STAND/KIOSK* | Places where you can buy snacks to take away. |
| *PIZZERIA* | Restaurants specializing in pizzas, sometimes also spaghetti and other Italian-type food. |
| *PANCAKE HOUSE/ CREPERIE* | A restaurant specializing in crêpes and pancakes with various sweet or savoury fillings. |
| *TABLE D'HÔTE RESTAURANT* | A restaurant serving complete meals with an appetizer, main course and a dessert at a fixed price. |
| *A LA CARTE RESTAURANT* | A fully-licensed restaurant with a complete, well-varied menu from which guests can choose the dishes they want. |
| *DANCING RESTAURANT* | Usually a fully licensed *à la carte* restaurant with dancing and perhaps other kinds of programme. |
| *COFFEE SHOP/ BRASSERIE* | Usually connected with a hotel. A place where guests can have breakfast or a quick meal at a moderate price. |
| *CARVERY* | A restaurant often connected with a hotel. Guests can carve for themselves as much as they want from roast joints at a fixed price. |
| *GRILL ROOM/ STEAK HOUSE* | Restaurants specializing in grilled steaks. |
| *'SPECIALTY' RESTAURANT 'THEME' RESTAURANT 'ETHNIC' RESTAURANT* | A restaurant with a special atmosphere created by décor, furnishing and a specific choice of dishes. Ethnic restaurants present the eating habits and culture of a certain nationality e.g. Chinese, French, Italian Russian etc. |
| *NIGHT CLUB* | A restaurant where guests normally come fairly late and stay until the small hours. Always with dancing and often also with floor shows and other entertainment such as roulette. |

# *Practice*

**Exercise I**   What types of restaurant would you recommend to the following people:

1   A young couple wanting food and some entertainment late at night.

2   A man wanting a meal in a place where he can meet some local people.

3   Someone wanting a quick, cheap meal.

4   A lady wanting to eat in a quiet atmosphere outdoors.

**Exercise II**   How does the system of restaurants differ in your country? Do you have other categories? Prepare a list of restaurant types and describe each.

# Personnel

## *Restaurant organization chart*

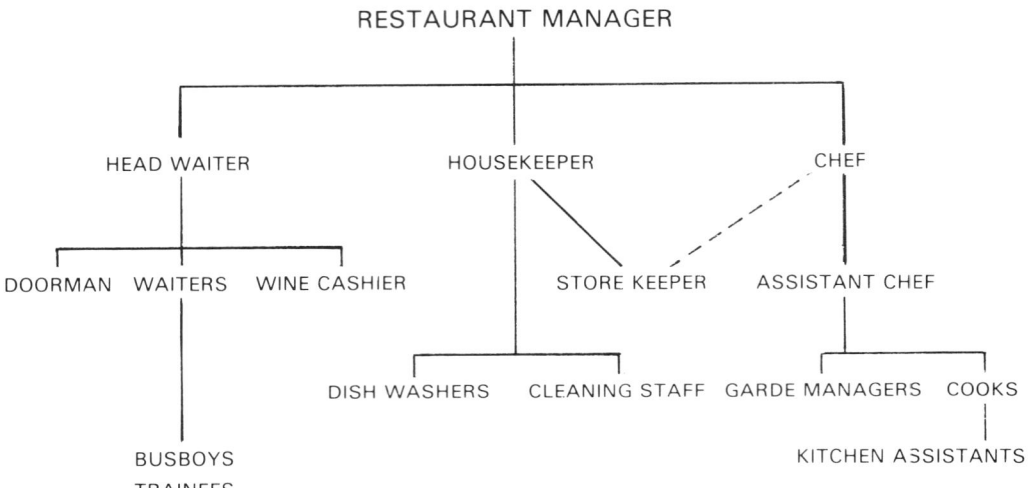

RESTAURANT MANAGER

HEAD WAITER      HOUSEKEEPER      CHEF

DOORMAN   WAITERS   WINE CASHIER      STORE KEEPER   ASSISTANT CHEF

DISH WASHERS    CLEANING STAFF   GARDE MANAGERS   COOKS

BUSBOYS
TRAINEES                     KITCHEN ASSISTANTS

*RESTAURANT MANAGER* is responsible for all the restaurant service and is in general charge of all persons connected with it. He quotes prices for daily menus and, in addition, makes arrangements for banquets and private parties.

*MAITRE D'HOTEL / HEAD WAITER* is in direct charge of either the whole of a small restaurant or a part of a larger one; he supervises the service, receives the guests and seats them. He may take the orders from the guests and pass them to the waiters.

*WAITER / WAITRESS* takes the guests' orders via a head waiter, otherwise direct from the guests, places the orders in the kitchen, assembles them, carries the food to the restaurant and serves the guests.

**BUSBOY/TRAINEE APPRENTICE** takes care of general cleanliness of the restaurant, carries away dirty dishes from the restaurant to the pantry, and replenishes the sideboard with additional dishes and cutlery. He assists those above him, may bring dishes from the kitchen, and sometimes helps with the serving.

**CHEF** supervises the preparation and service of the food from the kitchen to the dining room. Arranges the menus. Tastes food for correct seasoning. Plans the cooking times for completion before dining-room service begins. Checks that the food is garnished properly.

**COOKS SAUCE COOK** makes soups and sauces for various dishes.

**VEGETABLE COOK** cooks all the vegetables.

**FISH COOK** prepares all fish dishes and very often egg dishes.

**COLD MEAT COOK/ GARDE MANAGER** is in charge of the preparation of all cold foods, e.g. *hors d'oeuvre,* cold meats, *canapés,* sandwiches, dressings and salads.

**PASTRY COOK** prepares all pastry, desserts, cakes and ices.

**BARMAN/ BARTENDER** is in charge of the bar area.

**BAR WAITER/ WAITRESS COCKTAIL WAITER/WAITRESS** serves drinks to the tables in the bar.

**WINE CASHIER/ DISPENSE BAR CASHIER/ DISPENSE BARMAN** distributes alcoholic beverages and receives the payments for them from the waiters.

**HOUSEKEEPER** is in charge of general cleanliness, linen, dishes, utensils and decorations. Sometimes also in charge of the allocation of duties and other questions concerning the staff.

5

# *Practice*

***Exercise I***   Fill in the appropriate personnel:

1   _____ distributes alcoholic beverages to the waiters.

2   _____ prepares *hors d'oeuvres* sandwiches, salads etc.

3   _____ checks that food is prepared properly

4   _____ helps those above him and carries used dishes.

5   _____ is responsible for the bar area.

6   _____ supervises the service and takes orders

7   _____ serve food to the customers.

8   _____ take care of general cleanliness and linen.

9   _____ prepares soups and sauces.

10  _____ is in charge of the whole restaurant.

***Exercise II***  How does the personnel system differ in restaurants in your country?

# Applying for a job

Here are some advertisements for staff vacancies in restaurants:

## EXECUTIVE CHEF

REQUIRED FOR BEAUTIFUL Country House Hotel/ Restaurant in Yorkshire. Applicants must have first class qualifications. This is an excellent opportunity for an ambitious and professional Chef, as the hotel is owned by one of the country's most prestigious restaurants. Excellent remuneration. Apply in writing:

**Mr. M. Reid,
Bontree Restaurant,
Church Street, Ilkley.**

## 2nd CHEF

### MALE/FEMALE

required. Permanent position. Live-in. Excellent wages and conditions. End of season bonus.

**Apply Manager or Tel. Stornoway 2604. Caberfeldh Hotel, Manor Park, Stornoway, Isle of Lewis.**

## ROCKWELL COLLEGE OF EDUCATION

Rochester Road, Rockwell, Kent RB7 3HD

### COOKS

Required for kitchens serving staff and students at College of about 800 students.

Weekly wage for 40 hour week £49.32. Weekend rates and overtime payable at N.J.C. rates.

Part-time appointments will be considered.

Applications to Senior Catering Officer in writing, stating age, experience and qualifications, and the names and addresses of two referees; or by telephone: 01 734 984, ext. 26.

## TWO EXPERIENCED WAITERS/WAITRESSES

references required for small restaurant Woodford Green, Essex. Five nights, 7.00 pm to 1 am for 23rd May. Good salary.

**Ring Mr Johnson
01 450 485**

or Apply to:

Mr J. Johnson
Bon Appetit
Markwell Ave
Woodford Green
Essex.

## THREE WAITERS

required (male/female)

to work in our 4 star hotel restaurant.

Applicants should have previous experience in a large restaurant. A five day week is worked.

*Apply:*

**Personnel Manager, Highcliff Hotel, West Cliff, Bournemouth.**

# *Practice*

**Exercise I**     Study the advertisements for job vacancies and the letter of application and then complete the following sentences:

1   With _____ to your advertisement in the '*Daily Globe*' I should like to _____ for the position of chef.

2   I am _____ in the _____ for a waiter which you advertised in the '*Daily Globe*'.

3   I _____ my curriculum vitae _____ with references from my present employer.

4   I hope you will be able to _____ me for this post and look forward to _____ from you.

5   If you are interested in my _____ and would like to see me, I should be pleased to _____ for an _____.

**Exercise II**     Using some of the words and expressions you have learned, write letter of application in reply to some of the advertisements.

Here is a letter of application for the job of waiter/waitress at the *Bon Appetit* restaurant.

14 Nursery Close
Pier Road
Littlehampton LH1 4PR

22 March 1981

Mr J Johnson
Bon Appetit
Markwell Ave
Woodford Green
Essex

Dear Sir

I am applying for the position of waitress advertised in the 'Daily Globe' on 20 March 1981. I enclose my curriculum vitae, together with references from my last employer and from the Hotel and Restaurant School where I trained. I very much hope you can consider me for this post.

Yours faithfully

*Elina Malinen*

Elina Malinen (Miss)

CURRICULUM VITAE


NAME                           Elina Malinen

DATE AND PLACE OF BIRTH        2 March 1958, Riihimäki

MARITAL STATUS                 Single

ARMY RANK                      ---

EDUCATION                      Riihimäki Comprehensive School
                               1964-73
                               Hotel and Restaurant School, Helsinki
                               1975-76

PRACTICAL EXPERIENCE           Kitchen assistant, January-June 1974
                               Waitress trainee, June-December 1976
                               at the Hotel Neptune
                               Waitress, Hotel Scandinavia 1977-1980

QUALIFICATIONS                 Secondary school certificate
                               Catering diploma

LANGUAGES                      Swedish (fluent), English (good)
                               German (satisfactory)

Elina Malinen was in fact invited for an interview at the *Bon Appetit* restaurant. Here is part of the interview:-

| | |
|---|---|
| *Johnson* | Good evening, Miss Malinen, Won't you sit down? |
| *Elina* | Good evening. Thank you. |
| *Johnson* | Now, I notice you left the Hotel Scandinavia in 1980. What are you now doing in England? |
| *Elina* | I'm spending a few months brushing up my English and getting to know the country better. |
| *Johnson* | And you want to work in England too. Why? |
| *Elina* | I'm keen on getting some experience abroad, and I like England and English people. |
| *Johnson* | Good. Now I see from the information you sent me that you've worked in your last employment for nearly four years. Was that a large restaurant? |
| *Elina* | Medium-size for Finland, about 40 tables. |
| *Johnson* | I see. Well, you'd find it rather different here. Ours is much smaller, we have only 10 tables. |
| *Elina* | That must be very cosy. |
| *Johnson* | We try to create a warm, intimate atmosphere. Now, as to the job, you would be expected to look after 5 tables normally, though we get in extra staff for peak periods. |
| *Elina* | I see. |
| *Johnson* | I'm the Restaurant Manager and Head Waiter, so you'd be working directly under me. You'd be responsible for bringing in the dishes from the kitchen, serving the drinks, and if necessary looking after the bills. So you'd be kept pretty busy. |
| *Elina* | I'm used to that. In my last position we were busy most of the time, especially in summer. |
| *Johnson* | Good. Now, is there anything you'd like to ask about the job? |
| *Elina* | Well, the usual question—what sort of salary were you thinking of paying? |
| *Johnson* | We pay our waiters £40 a week, and you would get your evening meal free. |
| *Elina* | I see. |
| *Johnson* | Now, you may have wondered why I asked you here so late in the day. The fact is, I would like to see you in |

11

action, so to speak. Would you be willing to act as a waitress here this evening for half-an-hour or so? Our first customer will be coming in, let me see, in about ten minutes' time.

*Elina*   Well, I'm free this evening otherwise.

*Johnson*   Good. And in return perhaps you will have dinner with us? Now, let me show you the kitchen first. This way, please . . . .

# *Practice*

### *Exercise I*

1   Why did Elina leave her job and come to England?
2   Do you think she would find the job at the *Bon Appetit* restaurant difficult or easy? Why?
3   What does the job entail?
4   What terms are being offered?
5   How does Mr Johnson intend to find out how good Elina would be?

### *Exercise II*

Divide into groups of candidates and interviewers and prepare your letter of application or your questions for the advertised vacancies at the *Highcliff Hotel.* Act out the interviews in turn using the appraisal sheets to assess the candidates. While watching each group, also use the interviewers' appraisal sheets to assess the interviewers. Compare and discuss your opinions afterwards.

---

CANDIDATE'S APPRAISAL SHEET

Award points from 4-0: 4 = Excellent, 3 = Good, 2 = Fair, 1 = Poor, 0 = Hopeless

Name: _____ Points

1   Did the candidate seem confident or nervous?

2   Was he polite or not?

3   Did he give a good general impression?

4   Did he appear to know his job?

5   Did he ask sensible questions?

Total (out of 20)

---

INTERVIEWERS' APPRAISAL SHEET

Points as above

Names: _____ Points

1   Did the interviewers take notes?

2   Did they get what they wanted?

3   Did they describe the restaurant and the job?

4   Did they give a chance to ask questions?

5   Was the general atmosphere pleasant?

Total (out of 20)

# *Useful Phrases*

The restaurant manager

The head waiter

The chef

The cashier

The wine waiter

You can apply to my previous employer for references.

I have my references with me.

I should be pleased to attend for an interview.

# Chapter 2
# *PROMOTING THE BUSINESS*

## A new restaurant

Look at these notices:-

### ONCE AGAIN THE LONDON TOWN RESTAURANT IS OPEN TO THE PUBLIC!

After careful restoration **THE LONDON TOWN** is open again throughout the year. As in its golden age, it offers a wide range of services.

### CAFE PICCADILLY

The Café Piccadilly opens early in the morning and provides a welcome break for shoppers. Just help yourself to tea, coffee and delicious cakes or sandwiches from the self service counter. At noon they wheel in the drinks trolley from which wines and liqueurs are served.

### WESTMINSTER BAR

In the evening the Café Piccadilly joins with the rest of the restaurant to become a bar lounge. Here you can enjoy a pleasant drink or dance to the music of a live band.

## VICTORIA AND ALBERT ROOMS

The Victoria Room is an elegant luncheon and evening restaurant with waiter service.
It continues into the Albert Room, which can easily be separated by a partition for private functions.

## CELLAR PUB

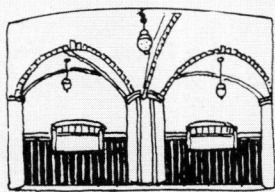

The Cellar pub is ideal for both the early shopper and the late night merrymaker fancying a light snack or something savoury.
The atmosphere is informal, with self-service and moderate prices.

## TERRACE RESTAURANT

In the summertime you can enjoy a meal or a refreshing drink in our shady terrace restaurant.

# *Practice*

### *Exercise I*

1 What has recently happened to *The London Town* restaurant?

2 What two types of service are provided?

3 What is the speciality of the Westminster Bar?

4 How do the Victoria and Albert Rooms differ from the other rooms?

5 What facilities does the Cellar Pub offer?

### *Exercise II*

Which of the facilities in the *London Town* restaurant would you consider suitable for the following customers?

1 A young couple wanting a late night snack.

2 A group of people who are looking for a comfortable place to talk and drink with some entertainment provided.

3 A guest wanting a quiet evening meal during the summer season.

4 A party celebrating a wedding anniversary and wanting to dine in style.

5 Two ladies wanting a mid-morning break from their shopping.

# A night-club

The BBC is doing a radio series called '*On the Town*', featuring interesting places of entertainment. Tonight is the turn of the *Casino de Pigalle*. Jenny Gates, the well-known radio interviewer, is talking to Barry Best, who manages the Casino.

| | |
|---|---|
| *Jenny* | And tonight, friends, our guest in the studio is a popular man from a popular place—Barry Best from the *Casino de Pigalle—oh là, là*! |
| *Barry* | Thank you Jenny for those kind words, and a very good evening to all of you. |
| *Jenny* | Now, tell me Barry, why should we come and visit the Casino? |
| *Barry* | I can give you five good reasons—you can dine, wine, dance see a really good floor show and play roulette in a genuinely swinging atmosphere. |
| *Jenny* | Great! Well, suppose we dine first. What do you have to offer us? |
| *Barry* | We offer a real gourmet's three-course dinner at a very reasonable price, with no membership or entrance fee required. |
| *Jenny* | No cover charge? |
| *Barry* | Not if you dine. And of course we accept credit cards. |
| *Jenny* | Okay. And now let's dine. |
| *Barry* | This way madam to our intimate lounge bar for a pre-dinner cocktail. |
| *Jenny* | Mmmm. That *does* sound tempting. |
| *Barry* | Where Tony Richardson and his piano will soothe your weary mind and stimulate your appetite. And your taste for our ample choice of very special wines. |
| *Jenny* | And how about my appetite for dancing? |
| *Barry* | Any time till 2.30 a.m. to two bands. |
| *Jenny* | And the floor-show? |
| *Barry* | All-star attractions, changed every week. This week it's Scott Connaris and his band, and I know I needn't say any more than that! |

*Jenny*  Lovely! And when is the roulette table uncovered?

*Barry*  At 9 p.m. sharp. You can play till midnight.

*Jenny*  Well, it all sounds very wonderful. Tell me, Barry, do you ever take a girl out for an evening on the town?

*Barry*  Do you mind if I answer that one, Jenny, after the programme?

**Broad Street**
**Tel: 64732**

**WINE** ❋
**DINE** *in elegant surroundings*
**DANCE** *with the stars*

* Open every night from 8 p.m. to 3 a.m.

* Pre-dinner cocktails in our intimate lounge bar with *Tony Richardson at the piano.*

* Gourmet dining with superb 3-course dinner at £10.

* Excellent choice of wines.

* Ever-changing star attractions.
  This week: International floor shows starring the world-famous *Scott Connaris with his band.*

* Cabaret at 11 p.m. and 1 a.m.

* Dancing to two bands until 2.30. a.m.

* Casino with roulette table open from 9 p.m. to midnight.

    No membership required, no entrance fee.
    Cover charge £3 for non-diners.
    Credit cards accepted.

# *Practice*

**Exercise I**  Complete the following publicity statements about the *Casino de Pigalle:*

1 You can _____ to the accompaniment of a different _____ every week.

2 There is no _____ if you dine at the Casino.

3 We provide a _____ for £10.

4 You can _____ from 9 pm till midnight.

5 The _____ is at 11 pm and 1 am.

**Exercise II**  Answer the following enquiries about the Casino:

1 When is the restaurant open?

2 What entertainment is there this week?

3 How much do we have to pay if we do not want to eat?

4 When does it close?

5 Do I have to be a member to get in?

**Exercise III**  Prepare some publicity information for a restaurant or night club of your own choice. You should consider the following features:-

Location

Opening times

Dining facilities (restaurants and snack bars)

Drinking facilities (bars, cocktail lounge)

Entertainment (music, floor-show, casino)

Charges

# *Useful phrases*

We offer a wide range of services

Live entertainment is provided every night

There is a cabaret twice nightly

We have an excellent choice of wines

Credit cards are accepted

A formal atmosphere

An informal atmosphere

No membership is required

Members only

# Chapter 3
# *SETTING THE SCENE*

## Cover for breakfast

Robert Farnham is training to be a waiter. Mr Hampden, the Head waiter, is telling him how to lay a cover for a continental breakfast.

| | |
|---|---|
| *Hampden* | First of all you take a paper tray cloth and spread it out neatly on the tray. Next you put a small side plate in the centre towards the bottom edge here with a side knife and napkin. Then on the right a breakfast cup, saucer and spoon, that's a teaspoon, of course. Next, on the left, you put the toast rack or sometimes when we have fresh rolls or croissants, a bread basket. |
| *Robert* | How do I know which one to put? |
| *Hampden* | It depends on the order. Next you need the preserve dish on a plate with a preserve spoon. In the left-hand corner we have the butter dish and butter knife. |
| *Robert* | Don't we ever use margarine? |
| *Hampden* | Good heavens, no. This is a first-class establishment. Let's get on. Now in the right-hand corner above the cup we put the sugar bowl. |
| *Robert* | What about the egg-cups? |
| *Hampden* | They come with the eggs from the kitchen if they are ordered. Now all we need is the coffee pot or teapot and next to it a hot water jug or jug with milk or cream. |
| *Robert* | That looks splendid, Mr Hampden. Thank you. |

Continental breakfast usually consists of croissants, rolls or hot toast, butter, preserves or marmalade and coffee or tea.

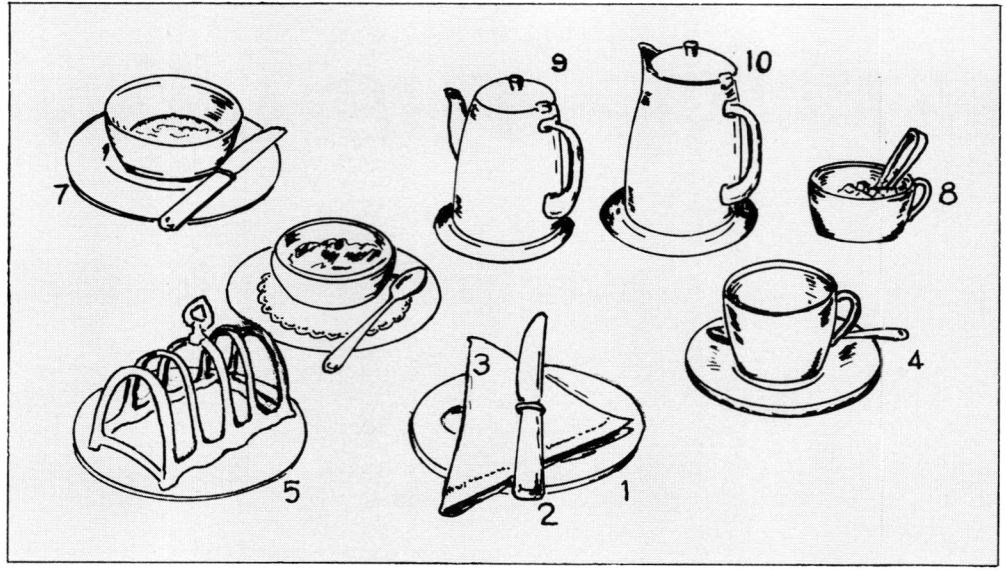

A breakfast tray laid for a continental breakfast

| 1 | Side plate |
|---|---|
| 2 | Side knife |
| 3 | Napkin |
| 4 | Breakfast cup, saucer and teaspoon |
| 5 | Toast rack or bread basket |
| 6 | Preserve dish with preserve spoon |
| 7 | Butter dish with butter knife |
| 8 | Sugar bowl |
| 9 | Coffee pot or teapot |
| 10 | Hot water jug or jug for cream or milk |

# Practice

**Exercise I**   See how much you can remember of the breakfast cover by completing the following sentences:-

1   You must remember to spread a _____ on the tray first.

2   A _____ is necessary for croissants or rolls and a _____ for toast.

3   The _____ must be placed on a _____ and is for jam, marmalade or honey.

4   The coffee pot or teapot should be provided with a _____ or _____.

5   A _____ is usually provided for guests to butter and cut their rolls or toast.

**Exercise II**   Take the parts of the head waiter and trainee waiter and practice the situation in pairs in your own words.

25

RE - C

# Cover for main meals

Robert Farnham next learns how to lay the table for dinner:

| | |
|---|---|
| *Hampden* | Well, we have to prepare for dinner this evening so let's begin over here at this large round table. |
| *Robert* | How many place-settings? |
| *Hampden* | Eight altogether. I see those fine linen tablecloths have already been spread out. Now in the middle first of all we have the service plate and serviette. On either side we place the dinner knife and fork. The fork on the left and the knife on the right. |
| *Robert* | What happens if someone is left-handed? |
| *Hampden* | That's his problem. Next we take the fish knife and fork and then the soup spoon on the right next to the fish knife. Now above the plate we need the dessert spoon and the fork; the spoon above the fork with the handle to the right. |
| *Robert* | Does the dessert fork have the handle to the left? |
| *Hampden* | Yes. Next we need a bread and butter plate with a side knife and some wine glasses. |
| *Robert* | How do I know whether it's a Hock, Burgundy or Claret glass? |
| *Hampden* | Look at the menu. This evening we have a Niersteiner with the smoked rainbow trout and a Gevrey-Chambertin with the reindeer. |
| *Robert* | So that's a Hock and a Burgundy. |
| *Hampden* | You are learning fast. Now we shall need salt and pepper shakers and a vinegar cruet. |
| *Robert* | What about the table number and menu card? |
| *Hampden* | Good. I nearly forgot those. Yes, they go here above the bread and butter plate, and perhaps we could put the ash tray over here on the right above the wine glasses. Now you carry on with the rest of the place-settings. |
| *Robert* | I'll have it done in no time, Mr Hampden, and thanks once again. |

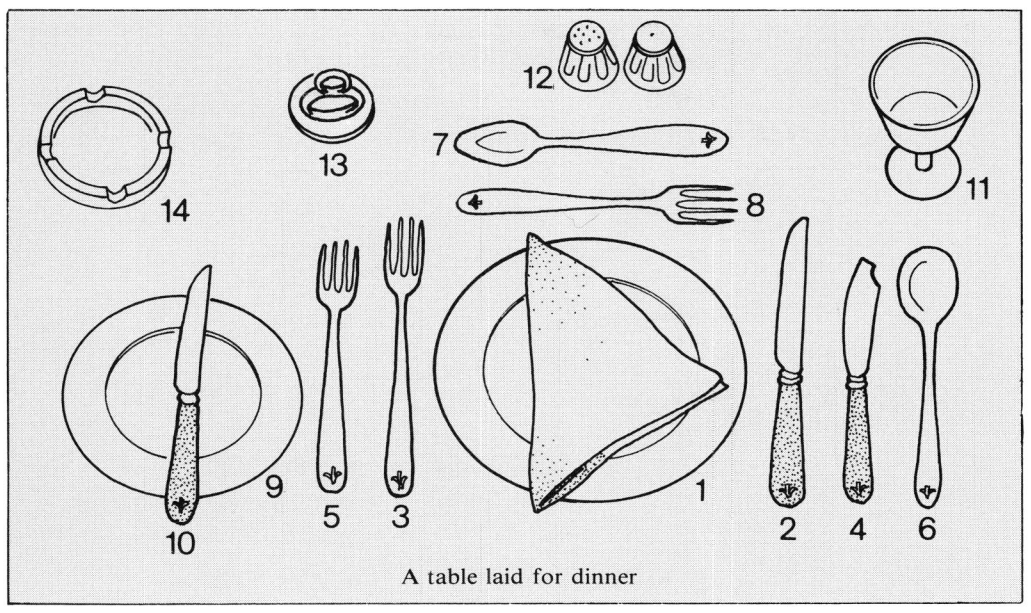

A table laid for dinner

| | | | |
|---|---|---|---|
| 1 | Service plate and serviette | 8 | Dessert fork |
| 2 | Dinner knife | 9 | Bread and butter plate |
| 3 | Dinner fork | 10 | Side knife |
| 4 | Fish knife | 11 | Wine glass |
| 5 | Fish fork | 12 | Salt and pepper |
| 6 | Soup spoon | 13 | Table number |
| 7 | Dessert spoon | 14 | Ash tray |

# Practice

***Exercise 1***  As before, try and complete these sentences:-

1  Where each person sits to eat is called a

_____

2  The _____ go on the left of the service plate with the _____ on the right.

3  A complete cover usually consists of _____ knives, _____ forks and _____ spoons.

4  Cutlery for the _____ course should be placed furthest away from the service plate.

5  The wine glasses usually go _____.

**Exercise II**   As before, take the parts of the head waiter and trainee and practise the situation in pairs.

**Exercise III**   Here are some of the items you need to know when laying or serving at a table. Match the objects with their names and functions from the following lists:

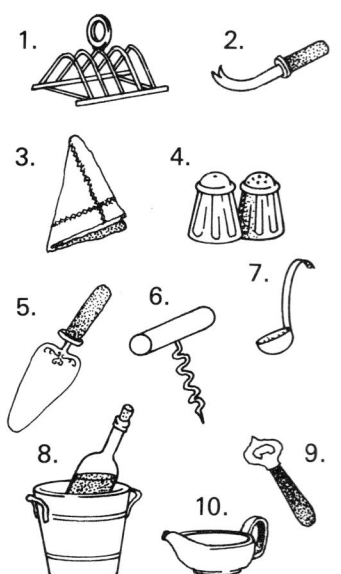

| | |
|---|---|
| serviette/napkin | opening wine bottles |
| cheese knife | opening tins or bottles |
| cruet set | serving salt and pepper |
| sauceboat | cooling wine |
| ice bucket | serving gravy |
| cake knife | serving soup |
| ladle | serving toast |
| bottle opener | cutting cheese |
| toast rack | serving gateau |
| corkscrew | wiping the mouth |

# Useful phrases

The tray has not been laid neatly enough
The table has to be set for (seven)
Where do you keep (the cruet sets)?
Where does (the serviette) go?
What wine glasses do we provide for (red wine)?
The (salt cellar) needs filling.

## Chapter 4

# *START THE DAY RIGHT*

## Continental and English breakfasts

Look at the Breakfast Menu of the *Basket* Restaurant. Here you can get an *à la carte* breakfast, a Continental breakfast or an English breakfast.

Here are two orders:

| | |
|---|---|
| *Woman* | I'd like the Continental breakfast please. |
| *Waiter* | Yes madam. What sort of fruit juice would you like to start with? |
| *Woman* | The pineapple juice. |
| *Waiter* | Would you prefer honey, marmalade or jam? |
| *Woman* | Oh, marmalade please. |
| *Waiter* | And what would you like to drink madam? |
| *Woman* | Coffee please, black coffee. |

| | |
|---|---|
| *Man* | May I have a look at the breakfast menu please? |
| *Waitress* | Here you are sir. |
| *Man* | Thank you. . . . I think I'll have the English breakfast. |
| *Waitress* | Yes sir. What would you like to start with? |
| *Man* | I'll start off with a glass of pineapple juice—no, wait a minute, I see there's cereal too. Do you have things like corn flakes? |

29

# BASKET

## BREAKFAST

Served from 7.00 a.m. — 10.30 a.m.
Sundays and Bank Holidays
8.00 a.m. — 11.00 a.m.

## ENGLISH

£1.25

Tomato, Prune or Pineapple Juice
or
Fresh Orange Juice or Fresh Grapefruit Juice
or
Porridge or Cereals of Your Choice

Two Eggs Cooked As You Wish with Bacon, Sausage, Mushrooms or Grilled Tomato

Panier of Fresh Breakfast Rolls, Hot Croissants and Toast served with Butter, Marmalade, Honey or Jam.

Tea, Coffee or Milk

## A LA CARTE

Tomato, Prune or Pineapple Juice:
*Small* £0.25 *Large* £0.40
Fresh Orange Juice or Fresh Grapefruit Juice *Small* £0.30 *Large* £0.50
Stewed Prunes or Figs £0.30
Chilled Seasonal Melon £0.50
Half a Grapefruit £0.30
Fresh Grapefruit Cocktail £0.35
Strawberries *(When in season)*
Raspberries *(When in season)*
A Choice of Fruit—
*per piece* £0.20
Yoghurt £0.25
Porridge or Cereals of Your Choice £0.20

Two Eggs Cooked as You Wish £0.40
Bacon, Sausage, Tomato and Mushrooms £0.40
A Three Egg Omelette of Your Choice £0.55
Ham Salad £1.00

Breakfast Sirloin Steak £1.50
A Pair of Kippers £0.70
Smoked Haddock and Poached Egg £0.80
Pancakes with Maple Syrup or Sugar and Lemon £0.60

Fresh Breakfast Rolls, Hot Croissants or Toast with Butter £0.17
Marmalade, Honey or Jam £0.15
Tea, Coffee or Milk £0.20

## CONTINENTAL

£0.87

Tomato, Prune or Pineapple Juice
or
Fresh Orange or Fresh Grapefruit Juice

Panier of Fresh Breakfast Rolls, Hot Croissants and Toast served with Butter, Marmalade, Honey or Jam.

Tea Coffee or Milk

Prices include Service Charge
Plus V.A.T. at Standard Rate

| | |
|---|---|
| *Waitress* | Yes, we have corn flakes, Rice Krispies or müsli. |
| *Man* | I'll have the Rice Krispies then. Now, let's see—ah, yes, the good old bacon and eggs and so on. |
| *Waitress* | Would you prefer mushrooms or grilled tomato, sir? |
| *Man* | Tomato I think. |
| *Waitress* | And would you like marmalade, honey or jam with your toast? |
| *Man* | Oh, definitely marmalade. That's the proper thing for a real English Breakfast, isn't it? |
| *Waitress* | That's right sir. And what would you like to drink? |
| *Man* | A nice big pot of tea, please. |

# *Practice*

**Exercise I**    Answer the following questions:

1  What does the European continental breakfast consist of?

2  What does the English breakfast consist of?

3  What did you have for breakfast this morning?

4  What do you think a good breakfast should be like?

5  In what way is the '*a la carte*' menu different?

**Exercise II**    Fill in the missing words:

1  Breakfast is served _____ 7 am _____ 10 am.

2  Would you _____ tea or coffee?

3  I'd like to pay. Could you please bring me the _____ ?

4  That'll be £2.50 plus _____.

5  Would you like _____ or _____ with your toast?

31

**Exercise III**    What would you say to a guest at the breakfast table if you wanted to know the following?

1    Which type of breakfast he wants.
2    What he would like to start with.
3    How he would like his eggs cooked.
4    What he would like with his eggs.
5    Whether he would like fruit juice or cereal.

**Exercise IV**    Here is another order but the waiter's part of the conversation is missing. See if you can complete it.

*Woman*    I'd like the English breakfast please.

*Waiter*    _____?

*Woman*    Orange juice please.

*Waiter*    _____?

*Woman*    Mushrooms, I think.

*Waiter*    _____?

*Woman*    Honey.

*Waiter*    _____?

*Woman*    No thank you. Just a glass of milk.

**Exercise V**    Practice giving and taking breakfast orders in pairs using the *Basket* Restaurant menu to help you.

# *Useful phrases*

What would you like to start with?

Would you like marmalade, honey or jam?

How would you like your eggs? Poached, scrambled, fried or boiled?

Hard or soft boiled?

There is a fixed price for the English and Continental breakfasts, all inclusive.

The continental breakfast consists of juice, toast and marmalade and coffee or tea.

At what time would you like your breakfast?

Would you prefer tea or coffee?

Would you like to have the Continental or the English breakfast?

# Chapter 5
# *HAVE YOU A TABLE?*

## Making reservations over the telephone

Here are two telephone conversations:

| | |
|---|---|
| *Manager* | *Apple Tree* Restaurant, good morning. |
| *Woman* | Can I speak to the Manager please? |
| *Manager* | Speaking. |
| *Woman* | I'd like to book a table for tomorrow lunchtime. |
| *Manager* | Yes madam, for how many will that be? |
| *Woman* | For seven. |
| *Manager* | And what time will you be arriving? |
| *Woman* | Oh, about twelve thirty I should think. |
| *Manager* | Table for seven at 12.30 on Wednesday. And what name was it please? |
| *Woman* | Leavens, Mary Leavens. |
| *Manager* | Very good madam. We look forward to seeing you. |
| *Woman* | Thank you. Goodbye. |
| *Manager* | Goodbye. |

---

| | |
|---|---|
| *Man* | Is that the *Barbecue* Restaurant? |
| *Waiter* | Yes sir. Can I help you? |
| *Man* | Could I speak to the Head Waiter please? |
| *Waiter* | I'm afraid he's not here just now. Could I take a message? |

|         |                                                                                      |
| ------- | ------------------------------------------------------------------------------------ |
| *Man*    | Yes. I ordered a table for 12 for dinner today, but I'm afraid I'll have to cancel it. |
| *Waiter* | What name was it please?                                                             |
| *Man*    | Bartleby, Nicholas Bartleby.                                                          |
| *Waiter* | I'm sorry, I'm afraid I didn't catch that. Could you spell it please?                 |
| *Man*    | Bartleby, B-A-R-T-L-E-B-Y.                                                            |
| *Waiter* | Very good Mr Bartleby. I'll make sure the Head Waiter gets the message.               |
| *Man*    | Thank you. Goodbye.                                                                   |
| *Waiter* | Goodbye.                                                                              |

# Practice

**Exercise I**  If you were answering reservation enquiries over the telephone in a restaurant, what would you say to customers to express the following?

1   You want to know how many people the reservation is for.

2   You want to know when the reservation is for.

3   You want to know the name the reservation should be under.

4   You didn't understand the customer's name.

5   You will pass the message to the head waiter.

**Exercise II**  Practise the following situations in pairs. Remember to put in all the necessary polite phrases for a telephone conversation.

1   The head waiter of the *Barbecue* Restaurant answers the telephone. The customer wants to book a table for the following day at 8 p.m. When asked for how many he says four, preferably a window table. He says his name is Southall and the head waiter asks him to spell it.

2   The same situation but the customer wants to cancel his table booking. He has a difficult name, Maugham. Make sure you get the day and time too.

3   This time the customer wants to speak to the manager, Mr Robins, but he's not available. So the head waiter takes a message that the manager should phone to. . . . (name and phone number).

4   A waiter answers the telephone but the customer wants the head waiter who is not there. The waiter offers to take a message but the customer wants to know when the head waiter will be back and says he will call again.

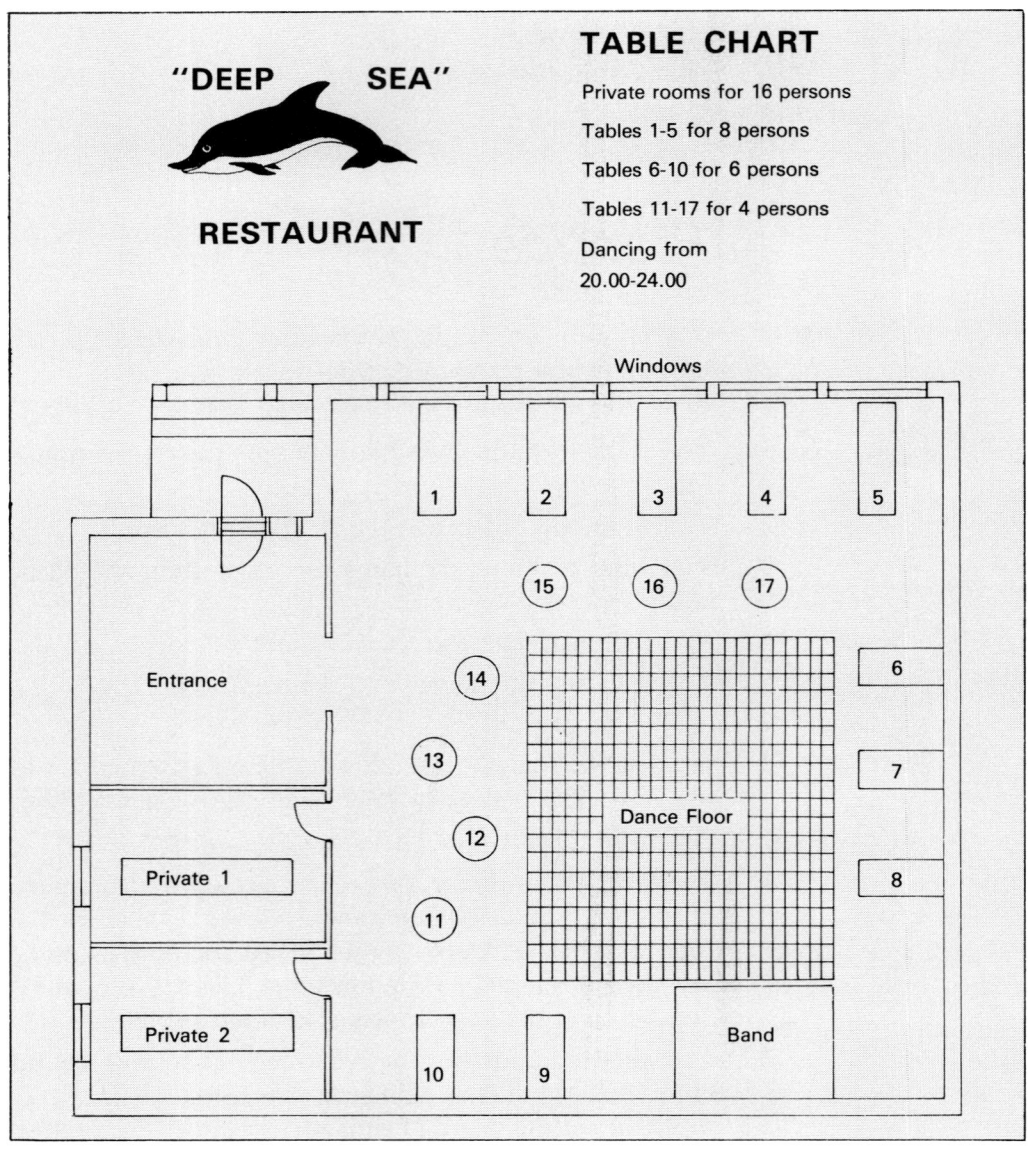

**"DEEP SEA"**

**RESTAURANT**

**TABLE CHART**

Private rooms for 16 persons

Tables 1-5 for 8 persons

Tables 6-10 for 6 persons

Tables 11-17 for 4 persons

Dancing from
20.00-24.00

Windows

Entrance

Private 1

Private 2

Dance Floor

Band

**DEEP SEA RESTAURANT**   **Reservations**   Monday Feb 29

Lunch 12-15

Table No.

| | Lunch | | | Dinner | |
|---|---|---|---|---|---|
| 1 | Williams | 13 30 | 1 | Watson | 19.00 |
| 2 | | | 2 | Jones | 18 30 |
| 3 | | | 3 | Hijab | 21.00 |
| 4 | Berner | 12.30 | 4 | | |
| 5 | Reinholdt | 14.00 | 5 | British Embassey | 20.00 |
| 6 | | | 6 | | |
| 7 | Delaney | 13.00 | 7 | | |
| 8 | | | 8 | Niemenen | 19.00 |
| 9 | | | 9 | | |
| 10 | Saarinen | 12.00 | 10 | Binham | 20.30 |
| 11 | Pratt | 13.00 | 11 | | |
| 12 | | | 12 | Murray | 21.30 |
| 13 | del Monte | 13.30 | 13 | | |
| 14 | | | 14 | | |
| 15 | Jackson | 12.30 | 15 | Leblanc | 18.00 |
| 16 | Hamilton | 14.30 | 16 | Carillo | 20.00 |
| 17 | | | 17 | | |
| Private 1 | Finner | 12.30 | Private 1 | Barker | 21.00 |
| Private 2 | | | Private 2 | | |

Dinner 18-22 (Closes 24)

Look at the Table Chart of the *Deep Sea* Restaurant. You'll see that there are 2 private rooms for a maximum of 16 persons, 5 tables for 8, 5 tables for 6, and 7 tables for 4 persons. There is dancing from 8 p.m. till midnight.

Now look at the head waiter's table reservations for Monday, February 29th. Lunch is from 12 midday till 3 p.m., and dinner is served from 6 p.m. until 10 p.m. Notice that some of the tables are already booked, both for lunch and dinner.

37

It's 11 a.m. on February 29th, only one hour till lunchtime. The head waiter's telephone starts ringing.

| | |
|---|---|
| *Head waiter* | *Deep Sea* Restaurant. Head waiter. Good morning. |
| *Woman* | I'd like to reserve a table for five. |
| *Head waiter* | And was that today, madam? |
| *Woman* | Of course. |
| *Head waiter* | At what time, madam? |
| *Woman* | Oh, about three o'clock I suppose. |
| *Head waiter* | I'm afraid we only serve lunch until 3 p.m., madam. |
| *Woman* | Oh well, 2 o'clock then, and it must be by a window. |
| *Head waiter* | Very good, and what name please? |
| *Woman* | Bellington, Mrs Martha Bellington. |
| *Head waiter* | Very good Mrs Bellington. A table for five at 2 p.m. today. |

| | |
|---|---|
| *Head waiter* | *Deep Sea* Restaurant. Good morning. |
| *Man* | Do you have a table for two this evening? |
| *Head waiter* | Certainly sir. At what time was it? |
| *Man* | What time does the band start playing? |
| *Head waiter* | At 8 p.m sir. |
| *Man* | Right. Make it 7.30 then, and near the dance floor if possible. |
| *Head waiter* | Very good sir. And what name please? |
| *Man* | Kryzkoviak |
| *Head waiter* | Could you just repeat that please? |
| *Man* | Kryzkoviak, that's Polish you know. K-R-Y-Z-K-O-V-I-A-K. |
| *Head waiter* | Yes. Thank you Mr Kryzkoviak. We look forward to seeing you. |

# *Practice*

*Exercise 1*    Assuming Table 3 was reserved for Mrs Bellington and Table 14 for Mr Kryzkoviak, you take the part of the head waiter in the following conversations. Remember to refer to your table reservations.

*Head waiter*   _____.

*Woman*   Good morning. Do you have a private room for 15 for lunch today?

*Head waiter*   _____?

*Woman*   12.30 if possible.

*Head waiter*   _____?

*Woman*   Mark it down for Spearhead Trips please.

*Head waiter*   _____.

*Woman*   Thank you. Goodbye.

*Man*   Good evening. Could you put me through to the *Deep Sea* Restaurant please?

*Head waiter*   _____.

*Man*   Ah, good. Listen. I'd like to book a table for 8 people please.

*Head waiter*   _____?

*Man*   For tonight.

*Head waiter*   _____.

*Man*   Oh, I see.

*Head waiter*   _____?

*Man*   I was hoping for something around about 8 o'clock.

*Head waiter*   _____.

*Man*   OK, 9 o'clock would be fine.

*Head waiter*   _____?

*Man*   Deleuse, D-E-L-E-U-S-E.

*Head waiter*   _____.

*Man*   Marvellous. Thank you. Goodbye.

**Exercise II** Practice more reservations like this in pairs. Remember to note down the reservations so you know which tables are still free.

# Useful phrases

When ⎫
How many ⎭ would that be for?

What time would you like to arrive?

What name is it please?

Very good (Madam). We look forward to seeing you.

I'm sorry I didn't quite catch that. Could you spell your name please?

I'm afraid we only serve (lunch) until (2.30).

I'm afraid we're fully booked at that time.

# Chapter 6
# *DINING OUT*

## Set lunch

Here is a simple set lunch menu:

October 20
Lunch
(12 noon — 2 pm)

Soup of the day
Egg mayonnaise

---

Plaice with french fries and peas
Lamb chops with boiled potatoes and peas

---

Apple pie with cream
Ice cream

---

Coffee

£4.50
Service & VAT
included

RE - D

Mr Radford has just dropped in for a quick lunch:-

| | |
|---|---|
| *Waitress* | A table for one, sir? |
| *Mr Radford* | Yes please. |
| *Waitress* | Are you having the set lunch? |
| *Mr Radford* | Yes. |
| *Waitress* | What would you like to start with? |
| *Mr Radford* | What's the soup of the day? |
| *Waitress* | Mushroom. |
| *Mr Radford* | Yes please. I'll have that. |
| *Waitress* | And for your main course? |
| *Mr Radford* | The plaice, I think, and apple tart to follow. |
| *Waitress* | Would you like something to drink with your meal? |
| *Mr Radford* | Yes. A lager please. |
| *Waitress* | Thank you |

# *Practice*

**Exercise I**   Take the part of the waiter in the following conversation.

| | |
|---|---|
| *Lady* | Good afternoon. Are you open for lunch? |
| *Waiter* | _____? |
| *Lady* | Just for me, please. |
| *Waiter* | _____. |
| *Lady* | Thank you. |
| *Waiter* | _____? |
| *Lady* | The egg mayonnaise, please. |
| *Waiter* | _____? |
| *Lady* | The lamb chops, I think. |
| *Waiter* | _____? |
| *Lady* | No thank you. Just some iced water. |

**Exercise II**   Practice giving and taking orders in pairs, using Mr Radford's menu to help you.

Here is a more elaborate menu:-

# The Harcourt Arms
# Stanton Harcourt
# Oxfordshire
## Oxford 881931

- Grilled king prawns with garlic bread and mayonnaise.
- Homemade stockpot soup.
- Liver pâté
- Deep fried sprats
- Avocado pear with vinaigrette or prawns

- Sirloin steak
- Roast duck with orange sauce
- Poussin and mushroom cream sauce
- Rack of lamb basted in honey & rosemary
- Baked Alaskan king crab in garlic butter and lemon juice
- Roast partridge & game gravy
- Rib of beef with bearnaise sauce

Served with green beans, carrots and jacket potatoes

Treacle tart with cream
Chocolate mousse

Coffee

Mr and Mrs Blackmore have just arrived at the *Harcourt Arms:*

|       |       |
|-------|-------|
| **Waiter** | Good afternoon. |
| *Mr Blackmore* | Good afternoon. I have a table booked for two under the name of Blackmore. |

| | |
|---|---|
| *Waiter* | Yes sir. Would you like to come this way? |
| *Mr Blackmore* | Thank you. |
| *Waiter* | Can I take your coat madam? |
| *Mrs Blackmore* | Thank you. |
| | |
| *Waiter* | Will this table do for you? |
| *Mr Blackmore* | That will be fine thanks. |
| *Waiter* | Would you like a drink before your meal? |
| *Mrs Blackmore* | Yes. A dry sherry please. |
| *Mr Blackmore* | Half a bitter for me. |
| | |
| *Waiter* | Are you ready to order? |
| *Mr Blackmore* | Yes I think so. |
| *Waiter* | What would you like for starters madam? |
| *Mrs Blackmore* | I can't decide. What do you recommend? |
| *Waiter* | Well, the prawns are always popular. The paté is very good. . . . |
| *Mrs Blackmore* | The prawns then please, for me. |
| *Waiter* | And for you sir? |
| *Mr Blackmore* | I think I'll try the soup. |
| *Waiter* | Very good sir. And to follow? |
| *Mrs Blackmore* | Rack of lamb, I think. |
| *Waiter* | And for you, sir? |
| *Mr Blackmore* | I'll have the steak. |
| *Waiter* | How would you like your steak done, sir? |
| *Mr Blackmore* | Medium rare please. |
| *Waiter* | Thank you. Would you like to see the wine list? |
| *Mr Blackmore* | Do you have house wine? |
| *Waiter* | Yes sir. Red or white? |
| *Mr Blackmore* | Do you have half bottles or half carafes? |
| *Waiter* | Yes sir. |
| *Mr Blackmore* | One of each then, please. |

# *Practice*

*Exercise I*   What would you say as the restaurant manager or waiter in the following situations?

1   Your guests arrive wearing coats.
2   You want to know if your guests would like an apéritif before their meal.
3   You want to know if your guests are ready to order their meal.
4   You want to know if your guests would like wine.
5   A guest asks you for your recommendations.

*Exercise II*   Using the same menu, practise giving and taking orders in pairs or in groups.

# **Dining** *à la carte*

John and Clare are having a celebration dinner at *The Hylands* restaurant:

| | |
|---|---|
| *John* | I thought that was a very interesting apéritif we had in the bar just now. I must ask them how it's made. |
| *Head Waiter* | Do you have a reservation, sir? |
| *John* | Yes, we booked some time ago. The name's Grant, John Grant. |
| *Head Waiter* | Ah, yes, Mr Grant. Would you like to come this way? Your table is over here by the window. |
| *John* | Thank you. |

| | |
|---|---|
| *Waiter* | Would you like to order now, sir? |
| *John* | Yes we would. Clare, have you made up your mind? |
| *Clare* | Yes, I'll begin with some salted salmon. |
| *John* | The marinated herring for me, please. |
| *Waiter* | I'm very sorry sir, but we have no more herring left. It's been a very popular dish this evening. |
| *John* | Oh dear. Well, I'll have the salmon too then. |
| *Waiter* | And for your main course? |
| *Clare* | What does the *béarnaise* sauce consist of? |
| *Waiter* | It's made principally from parsley, tarragon and vinegar, beaten with egg yolk. |
| *Clare* | There's no garlic in it? |
| *Waiter* | No madam. |
| | I'll have the fillet of beef then, with cauliflower. |
| *Waiter* | Very good madam. And for you, sir? |
| *John* | The escalope of veal *à la Oscar*. That sounds interesting What vegetables do you recommend to go with it? |
| *Waiter* | How about boiled potatoes and asparagus? |
| *John* | That will do fine. |
| *Waiter* | Would you like to choose a wine sir? |
| *John* | Why not; we're celebrating. |

---

| | |
|---|---|
| *Waiter* | Have you chosen your wine, sir? |
| *John* | Yes. We'll have a half bottle of white Bordeaux to start with, please and then a bottle of St Emilion. |
| *Waiter* | Certainly sir. |

Here is the menu and wine list they had:

# THE *HYLANDS*

## MENU

### Appetizers

Herring à la Russe
Salted salmon with poached eggs
Marinated rolls of Baltic herring
Prawn cocktail
Melon (when in season)

### Soups

Consommé
Asparagus
French onion

### Fish dishes

Poached salmon
Grilled whitefish with horseradish butter
Pikeperch Walewska au gratin

### Meat dishes

Fillet of beef with béarnaise sauce
Sirloin steak
Escalope of veal au gratin with creamed mushrooms
Pork chop with mustard sauce
Roast lamb with mint sauce
Calf liver anglaise

### Poultry dishes

Chicken casserole with rice
Snow grouse

### Vegetables

Mushrooms
Cauliflower
Asparagus
French fried potatoes
New potatoes
Brussel sprouts
Green peas

### Desserts

Ice cream
Sherry trifle
Fruit salad
Fresh strawberries and cream
Cheese

## WINE LIST

### Red Burgundy

Beaujolais AC
Cotès de Beaune Villages
Nuits St Georges

### White Burgundy

Chablis AC
Pouilly Vimzelles
St Veran

### Red Bordeaux

St Emilion AC
White Bordeaux

### White Bordeaux

Graves AC
Premières Côtes de Bordeaux

### German wines, Hock & Mosel

Goldener Oktober Liebfraumilch
Bereich Nierstein
Blue Nun
Bereich Berkastel

# Practice

**Exercise I**    Make suitable dishes from the following lists. Choose items from list *B* to go with items from list *A*

| A | B |
|---|---|
| Beef | Cream |
| Lamb | Game gravy |
| Fresh strawberries | Mint sauce |
| Plaice | Tartare sauce |
| Prawns | Mayonnaise |
| Roast duck | Orange sauce |
| Roast partridge | Bearnaise sauce |

**Exercise II**    Arrange the following dishes into a menu of starters, fish, meat, poultry, vegetables and dessert. Try not to look at John and Clare's menu until you have finished.

| | |
|---|---|
| Cheese | Escalope of veal |
| French onion soup | Grouse |
| Melon | Chicken casserole |
| Roast lamb | Pork chop |
| Peas | Mushrooms |
| Sherry trifle | |

**Exercise III**    Using John and Clare's menu, practise giving and taking orders in pairs or in groups.

# Useful phrases

Have you made a reservation sir?

Would you like to come this way, please?

May I take your coats?

Would you like a drink before your meal?

Are you ready to order?

What would you like to start with?

And to follow?

How would you like your steak done?

Would you like to see the wine list?

I'm afraid we have none left.

# Chapter 7
# *QUICK MEALS AT ALL TIMES*

## The snack bar

This is a conversation between two customers and the waiter at the *Happy Hamburger*:

|  |  |
|---|---|
| *Waiter* | Can I take your orders please? |
| *Man* | Yes. A Maxi Quarterpounder for me please. With chips. |
| *Waiter* | Anything else sir? |
| *Man* | A banana long boat, I think. |
| *Waiter* | What would you like to drink with your meal? |
| *Man* | Can I have a beer? |
| *Waiter* | I'm sorry sir, we are not licensed to sell alcohol. |
| *Man* | A cold milk then please. |
| *Waiter* | And for you, sir? |
| *2nd man* | I'll have the cheeseburger with a green salad please. |
| *Waiter* | And to follow? |
| *2nd man* | I'll decide later. |
| *Waiter* | And to drink? |
| *2nd man* | Cola please. |

Here is a menu at the *Happy Hamburger* snack bar:

# HAPPY HAMBURGER

## Maxi Quarterpounder  66p
* Quarter pound pure beef hamburger steak served in a toasted bun with fried onions and lettuce.

with chips **91p**

## Special Kingsize  80p
Two pure beef hamburger steaks with fried onions, in a toasted bun with lettuce and tomato, topped with melted cheese.

with chips **105p**

## Hamburger  35p
The pure beef hamburger in a toasted bun served with fried onions.

## Cheeseburger  46p

## Eggburger  51p

## Egg 'n' Baconburger  51p
A delicious Baconburger with a fried egg served on an open toasted bun.

## Portion of Chips
(Served with above) **25p**

## Hamburger Brunch  84p
Two pure beef hamburgers steaks served with fried onions and a portion of chips.

## House Salad  98p
Two hamburger steaks with fried onions served with lettuce and tomato, and a helping of vegetable salad.

* Approx. uncooked weight

## Hamburger Grill  84p
Hamburger steak with a Bender frankfurter served with fried onions, tomato, pickle and a portion of chips.

| | |
|---|---|
| EGG AND PORTION OF CHIPS | 45p |
| TWO EGGS AND PORTION OF CHIPS | 65p |
| GREEN SALAD | 50p |

## Special Grill  78p
Hamburger steak with a Bender frankfurter and fried onions, a fried egg, tomato, pickle, and a portion of chips.

## The International Grill  117p
One pure beef hamburger steak, a Bender frankfurter and a delicious Baconburger, served with fried onions, a portion of chips, tomato, lettuce and pickle.

## Baconburger Grill  84p
A delicious Baconburger, and a Bender frankfurter served with tomato, pickle and a portion of chips.

## Baconburger Special Brunch
Two delicious Baconburgers and a fried egg served with a portion of chips.

## Bender Brunch  84p
Two delicious Bender frankfurters served with fresh tomato, pickle and a portion of chips.

# HAPPY HAMBURGER

## Fish Brunch 84p
Two golden fried fish portions with tartare sauce and a portion of chips.

## Fish Salad 98p
Two fish portions with tartare sauce served with lettuce and tomato, and a helping of vegetable salad.

## Children's Brunch 50p
One hamburger steak of Bender frankfurter or Baconburger or fish portion with a portion of chips.

CHEESE EGGBURGER 62p
Please note that there is a minimum charge of 40p at Management's discretion.

## Ice Cream Portion 25p

## Chocolate Nut Sundae 30p
Ice cream covered with smooth chocolate sauce, topped with chopped nuts and a wafer biscuit.

## Strawberry Sundae 45p
Strawberries, ice cream and wafer.

## Fruit and Nut Sundae 40p
Ice cream with fruit cocktail, topped with chopped nuts and a wafer biscuit.

## Brown Derby 35p
A doughnut ring smothered with ice cream, covered with chocolate sauce and sprinkled with chopped nuts.

## Knickerbocker Glory 50p
A long luscious combination of strawberries, fruit cocktail and ice cream.

## Banana Long Boat 50p
A whole banana, split lengthwise, with fruit cocktail and a jumbo-size portion of ice cream.

## Whippsy 30p
Thick tasty milk shake with ice cream: strawberry, lime, chocolate, banana and vanilla flavours.

## Ice Cream Float 28p
A refreshing cola with ice cream.

## Sweets

| | |
|---|---|
| GATEAU or FRUIT FLAN | 30p |
| RUM BABA or APPLE SLICE | 30p |
| CHEESECAKE | 35p |

## Hot and Cold Drinks

| | | | |
|---|---|---|---|
| TEA | 13p | HOT CHOCOLATE | 22p |
| COFFEE | 18p | COLA | 18p |
| MILK | 15p | SPARKLING DRINKS | 18p |
| HORLICKS | 22p | ORANGE | 16p |
| LEMON TEA | 18p | | |

# *Practice*

**Exercise I**    1   How much will the meals ordered above come to?

                2   Why can't the man have a beer?

                3   What dessert is the second man going to have?

                4   Which of the two men is the hungrier?

**Exercise II**    Here is another conversation at the *Happy Hamburger* but this time the waiter's part is missing. See if you can complete it.

*Waiter*     _____?

*Woman*     Yes, I think so. Can I have the Baconburger Grill please?

*Waiter*     _____?

*Woman*     No, I don't think so. Well, maybe a green salad.

*Waiter*     _____?

*Woman*     A cup of tea please.

*Waiter*     _____?

*Woman*     I'll try the gateau, please.

**Exercise III**    Study the menu carefully and answer the following customers' questions:

      1   What is in the Maxi Quarterpounder?

      2   Have you any children's helpings?

      3   I'm not very hungry. Could you recommend a salad or something?

      4   Have you any fish dishes?

      5   What is your most expensive dish? What is in it?

      6   I've only got 45p and I'm very hungry. Can I get anything to eat with that?

      7   I'd like to have an enormous ice-cream portion. What do you recommend?

      8   Have you any milk shakes?

      9   I'd like a cup of coffee and something nice and sweet with that. What do you recommend?

    10   What does the fruit and nut sundae consist of?

# Automatic vending

Automatic vending means the supply of food and drinks both hot and cold, usually through coin-operated machines. They are mostly used in industrial and transport catering. These machines are found in canteens, schools, factories, garages, hospitals, hotels etc. They relieve some of the pressure of work on the waiters, kitchen staff, counter-hands and cashiers. This is especially true where a limited range of snacks and hot or cold drinks is required.

Some advantages of automatic vending machines:

> They provide a round-the-clock, 24 hour-service.
>
> Automatic vending allows standardised portion control and standard quality.
>
> Food cost control becomes more effective.
>
> They save labour costs.
>
> Drinks are always fresh and piping hot or ice cold.
>
> Automatic vending machines can be used together with the microwave oven. The snacks and meals are kept in refrigerated compartments. When the customer has chosen his meal he places it in a microwave oven to be reheated.
>
> Wastage can be cut to a minimum.

Among the most popular vending machines are those offering black or white coffee, with or without sugar. Also tea with the same combinations and hot chocolate are great favourites. The same machine may also provide cold soft drinks.

Other frequently-used types of vending machines include the following:

> hot food vendors
> refrigerated food vendors
> confectionery machines
> cigarette machines

Nowadays automatic vending is a necessity as part of the food service industry and will gain more and more importance in the future.

53

# Practice

**Exercise I**  Study the information on automatic vending and complete the following sentences:

1  Automatic vending machines _____ food and drinks on the insertion of the correct _____.

2  They can be more economical than snack bars because they reduce the cost of _____.

3  _____ they _____ out of order, they can serve snacks and drinks all the time.

4  They are mostly used in _____.

5  They can even _____ food by the use of _____.

**Exercise II**  What do you think are the advantages of vending machines? If you were the catering manager in a factory, educational institution or hotel, to what extent would you like to see these machines in use?

# Useful phrases

What would you like to drink with your meal?
We are not licensed to sell alcohol.
That comes to· £5.50 in all
That will be £5.50 all together

# Chapter 8
# *PAYING THE BILL*

| | |
|---|---|
| *Mr Hanson* | Could I have my bill please? |
| *Waitress* | Yes sir. One moment please. |
| | (she brings the bill and the customer looks at it carefully) |
| *Mr Hanson* | Could you kindly explain this to me? What is item 6? |
| *Waitress* | Perhaps I could go through it for you. The first item is the cover charge. Number 2 is the beer. Then your starter, your main course and the vegetables. The main course was 4.50 not 3.50, so item 6 is the difference. |
| *Mr Hanson* | Oh, I see. But how was I expected to know that? |
| *Waitress* | Yes sir. They are a bit hard to follow sometimes. Number 8 is your dessert and number 9 the cigarettes. Oh, and number 7 is your second beer. |
| *Mr Hanson* | And what about the service, is that included? |
| *Waitress* | Yes, that's marked down here, 10 per cent service. |
| *Mr Hanson* | Good. Thank you. Now, can you take my credit card? |
| *Waitress* | I'm afraid we don't accept credit cards. |
| *Mr Hanson* | Oh dear. What about a cheque with a banker's card? |
| *Waitress* | Yes sir. That will be all right. |

Here is another conversation:

| | |
|---|---|
| *Customer* | Can you bring me the bill please? |
| *Waiter* | Certainly sir. (He brings the bill) |
| *Customer* | I think there has been a mistake. |
| *Waiter* | I'm sorry sir. What seems to be the trouble? |
| *Customer* | I think you have charged me twice for the same thing. |

Here is Mr. Hanson's bill

| | | | | 047045 |
|---|---|---|---|---|

RESTAURANT

# Atlantica
**tel: 57.34.28**

| Table | 6 | Persons | 1 | Date | 21 7 |
|---|---|---|---|---|---|

| | | |
|---|---|---|
| 1 | Cover | .60 |
| 2 | Beer | .85 |
| 3 | Starter | 1.50 |
| 4 | M.Course | 3.50 |
| 5 | Veg | 35 |
| 6 | | 1.00 |
| 7 | Beer | 85 |
| 8 | Dessert | 2.00 |
| 9 | Cig | .75 |
| 10 | | |
| 11 | | |
| 12 | | |
| 13 | | |
| 14 | | |
| 15 | | |

| | | |
|---|---|---|
| Total | 11 | .40 |
| % | 1 | .14 |
| | 12 | .54 |

56

| | Look, the figure of 5.50 appears here and then again here. |
|---|---|
| *Waiter* | I'll just go and check it for you sir. |
| | (He returns a few minutes later) |
| | Yes sir, you are quite right. The cashier made a mistake. I think you will find it correct now. |
| *Customer* | Thank you. |
| *Waiter* | We do apologize about this sir. |
| *Customer* | That's all right. No harm done. Now, can I pay by traveller's cheques? |
| *Waiter* | Certainly sir. We'll give you the change in local currency if that's all right. |
| *Customer* | You needn't worry about that. There won't be much change out of $25. |
| *Waiter* | Thank you sir. That's most kind of you. |

# Practice

| *Exercise I* | What would you say as the waiter in the following situations? |
|---|---|
| 1 | The customer asks for his bill. |
| 2 | The customer does not understand his bill. |
| 3 | The customer thinks there is a mistake in the bill. |
| 4 | You want to know how the customer wishes to pay. |
| 5 | The customer asks if he can pay by credit card. |

| *Exercise II* | Take the part of the waiter and complete this conversation: |
|---|---|
| *Customer* | Bring me the bill please. |
| *Waiter* | _____ (He brings the bill) |
| *Customer* | It seems rather expensive for what I have had. |
| *Waiter* | _____? |
| *Customer* | Well, I've only had 3 courses and a bottle of wine and |

|  |  |
|---|---|
|  | there are 6 separate items costed here. |
| *Waiter* | _____ |
| *Customer* | Thank you. I think he will find there is a mistake or two at least.<br>(The waiter returns from seeing the cashier) |
| *Waiter* | _____. |
| *Customer* | Really? Would you mind explaining it to me? |
| *Waiter* | _____ |
| *Customer* | Oh, I see. The cover charge and vegetables are extra are they? And what about this item? |
| *Waiter* | _____. |
| *Customer* | Oh, I thought service was included. Never mind. Can I pay you in dollars? |
| *Waiter* | _____. |
| *Customer* | All right. I've got some traveller's cheques actually. |

**Exercise III** Prepare and practise conversations of your own between the customer and the waiter. Make up your own bills for each situation.

# Useful phrases

to pay: in cash
by traveller's cheque
in foreign currency
by credit card

Credit cards are not accepted.

We can take a cheque with a banker's card.

Do you want it all on the same bill or do you want to pay separately?

There is a cover charge.

Service is included.

What seems to be the trouble?

I think you'll find that is correct.

## Chapter 9

# *CAN I SEE THE MANAGER?*

## Politely dealing with complaints

Remember the purpose of a restaurant is to encourage customers to enter, enjoy their meal and spend their money. However, some difficulties may arise and you have to deal with them tactfully. Here are some examples:

| | | |
|---|---|---|
| *1. Man* | Do you have a table for four? |
| *Head waiter* | I'm afraid the whole restaurant is reserved tonight. Perhaps you would like to try the '*Good Taste*' Restaurant just round the corner? |

---

| | |
|---|---|
| *2. Woman* | We've booked a table for eight. The name is Darlington. |
| *Head waiter* | Yes madam. One moment please. I'm afraid there's no table reservation marked in that name, madam. |
| *Woman* | But I phoned myself only this afternoon and I was promised a window table. |
| *Head waiter* | I see. There must be some mistake, madam. Ah, we could give you a pleasant table in the Blue Room, though I'm afraid it isn't a window table. |
| *Woman* | Well, I suppose we'll have to manage with that, but I must tell you I'm disappointed with your service. |
| *Head waiter* | I'm very sorry indeed that this should have happened, |

madam, but I assure you we will make every effort to make your evening here a pleasant one.

_____

3. **Man** Waitress! This meat is like old leather! It's enough to break every tooth in your head.

**Waitress** Perhaps you'd like to change your order, sir. The sirloin is very tender.

_____

4. **Woman** This coffee is practically cold.

**Waiter** I am sorry madam. I'll bring you a fresh pot straight away.

_____

5. **Man** I'll take the Romany Beef.

**Waitress** I'm very sorry sir, the Romany Beef is not being served any longer. Perhaps you'd like to try our speciality the *Entrecôte Bordelaise*. I can thoroughly recommend it.

_____

6. **Man** Look here, that's chicken. I ordered fish, the Rainbow Trout Normandy.

**Waitress** Of course you did sir. I'm so sorry. I'll bring you your rainbow trout immediately sir.

_____

7. **Woman** John, look what that waiter's gone and done! Spilt soup all over my new dress!

**Waiter** I'm terribly sorry madam. Perhaps if I could sponge it with a little warm water. . .

**Man** Leave it alone man, you'll only make it worse.

**Woman** I want to speak to the Manager!

**Waiter** Very good madam.

**Manager** I do apologize for this unfortunate accident, madam. If you would like to have the dress cleaned and send the bill to us, we will be happy to take care of it.

**Woman** Oh no, it doesn't matter. Forget it. It probably won't stain very much.

_____

8. **Man** Waiter, this just won't do. This wine's got a most peculiar flavour.

**Waiter** Yes sir. I'll take it back. Perhaps you would like to choose another wine instead, sir?

9. *Man*   Three gin and tonics please.

*Waitress*   I'm sorry sir, but we're not allowed to serve drinks before 12 o'clock midday. Would you like me to bring you something else? Some coffee?

———

10. *Man*   Waiter, this table-cloth is a disgrace. It's covered with soup stains.

*Waiter*   Oh, I'm so sorry sir, it should have been changed before. If you'll just wait one moment . . .

———

11. *Woman*   Look at these glasses, this one's even got lipstick on it.

*Waiter*   I'm very sorry, madam, I'll bring you clean ones right away.

———

12. *Man*   Head waiter, I want to have a word with you.

*Head waiter*   Yes sir. Is there something wrong sir?

*Man*   Something wrong? I should think there is something wrong. My wife and I have been kept here waiting nearly an hour for our meal!

*Head waiter*   I'm terribly sorry about that sir. Our staff has been kept unusually busy this evening. I'll see to it personally myself. Now, if you wouldn't mind just telling me what you ordered.

———

13. *Man*   Waiter. I can't quite understand how you manage to get 10 marks plus 12 marks plus 65 marks 50 pennies to add up to 177 marks 50 pennies.

*Waiter*   One moment, I'll just check it sir. You're quite right, sir. I can't understand how such a mistake could have been made. I do apologize sir.

# *Practice*

**Exercise I**  Complete the following sentences:-

1  I'm _____ there isn't a table free till 10pm.

2  I'm sorry that this unfortunate _____ should have arisen.

3  We shall make every _____ to make your evening a pleasant one.

4  We do _____ for this inconvenience.

5  I am sorry, sir. I'll bring you another bottle _____ .

**Exercise II**  If you were the head waiter or manager or a restaurant what would you say in the following situations:

1  A party of guests want a table but the restaurant is full.

2  A guest complains that the bill is not correct.

3  The waiter has spilt some red wine on a gentleman's suit.

4  A guest wants roast turkey but there isn't any left.

5  A guest complains that the white wine is not chilled enough.

**Exercise III**  For which complaints would you say the following:

1  Certainly sir. Right away.

2  I'm very sorry madam, but we cannot allow this.

3  That would be rather difficult, I'm afraid sir.

4  I do appreciate that, madam, but I'm afraid we just don't have any left.

5  There seems to have been a misunderstanding. Could I suggest this one instead?

**Exercise IV**  Prepare complaints and polite ways of dealing with them and practice the situations in pairs.

# *Useful phrases*

Is anything wrong, madam?

Excuse me, but could you tell me what the trouble is, sir?

I'm afraid we don't have any just now.

I'm afraid that is not possible, madam.

That's rather difficult I'm afraid, sir.

We're rather full this evening I'm afraid.

I'm sorry madam, but. . .

I'm extremely sorry to hear that.

I'm very sorry sir, but we are obliged to observe the regulations.

I'm so sorry madam, there must be some mistake.

I do hope you will accept our apologies.

I do apologize for this unfortunate incident.

I'm sure you understand.

We'll attend to it right away.

We will certainly see what we can do about it, sir.

I'll see that it's changed right away, madam.

I'll have it seen to immediately.

# Chapter 10

# *SPECIAL DIETS*

## Religion forbids

John Andrews, a reporter from the British periodical *Caterer and Hotelkeeper* is writing a series of articles on 'Eating out in Europe'. Here he is interviewing Pieter de Ruiter, *chef de cuisine,* of a new hotel restaurant in Amsterdam.

*John*    I understand that apart from serving a wide variety of international dishes and specialities, you also cater for various religions and also people suffering from diabetes and gastric ulcers.

*Pieter*    That's quite correct. We aim to satisfy all our customers whatever their religion or state of health. Although there are quite a number of vegetarian restaurants springing up, there seems to be a lack of places offering special menus or even diet plates.

*John*    What are the problems involved in preparing meals for Moslems and Hindus, for example?

*Pieter*    Well, of course, first of all, Moslems, that is all Moslems, are forbidden to eat pork, bacon, ham or any foods containing pork in any form. Nor may they eat crabs, lobsters, shrimps or eels.

*John*    But surely that was just a custom evolved to avoid food poisoning in hot desert countries, wasn't it?

*Pieter*    Not only that. It is part of their faith and culture. After all, how many Christians would be happy to eat horse, cat or even mice?

*John*    Are the Hindus the same?

*Pieter*    Hindus do not eat beef or veal which unfortunately cuts out some of our superb dishes. But we have a large selection of special Indian fare.

*John*  Isn't it a bit off-putting to have people asking you to explain the origins of stews, pies and sausages?

*Pieter*  It is no more disconcerting than the Greek habit of coming straight into the kitchen to see what is on the menu. After all we have nothing to hide.

*John*  And how about '*kosher*' food?

*Pieter*  I must admit Jewish catering is much more complicated, following as it does the strict dietary laws and traditions laid down according to the Jewish religion.

*John*  What sort of problems come up there?

*Pieter*  First of all, blood must not be eaten and that means that animals have to be slaughtered in such a way that the blood is completely drained out of the animal. There again Jews are not allowed to eat the meat of animals which have no cloven hooves or do not chew the cud.

*John*  So that cuts out pork, too. How about oxtail soup?

*Pieter*  The hindquarters of animals are also forbidden. Another prohibition is the use of milk and meat together. Staff are not allowed to mix meat and milk equipment either in the kitchen or the food service area and after a meat meal Jews are not permitted milk foods for 4 hours.

*John*  How about egg dishes?

*Pieter*  They are allowed. To start the meal you can have a vegetable soup and fish for the main course avoiding skate and turbot of course, because fish must have fins and scales. The dessert need cause you no problems as you don't have to avoid cream as you have not served meat.

*John*  What about the fats used in the preparation of the food. Lard and dripping are presumably out, aren't they?

*Pieter*  Yes. We have to use butter or a vegetable oil.

# Practice

*Exercise I*

1 What are Moslems forbidden to eat?

2 Why are they not allowed to eat these foods?

3 What are Hindus not allowed to eat?

4 What do you know about the significance of animal blood in Jewish catering?

5 How about the combination of meat and milk in *kosher* catering?

*Exercise II*

Classify the following foodstuffs into the religions that forbid them:

| | |
|---|---|
| Blood | Bacon |
| Pork | Veal |
| Beef | Ham |
| Lard | Shellfish |
| Milk and meat products together | Animals' hindquarters |

*Exercise III*

Suggest suitable menus for a Moslem, a Hindu or a Jew eating in your restaurant.

# Health problems

Here are three special diets for diabetics, people with stomach trouble and weight-watchers:

# For Diabetics

*BREAKFAST*
Orange juice
Wholemeal roll
Cheese
Hot Chocolate (unsweetened)

*MORNING SNACK*  Half an orange

| | |
|---|---|
| *LUNCH* | Grilled escalope of veal<br>Boiled potatoes<br>Boiled carrots<br>Green salad with lemon juice |
| *AFTERNOON SNACK* | Cheese and biscuits |
| *DINNER* | Vegetable soup<br>Hot open sandwich with cheese and ham |
| *EVENING SNACK* | Glass of milk or<br>Hot chocolate (unsweetened) |

# *For ulcer sufferers*

| | |
|---|---|
| *BREAKFAST* | Hot cereals with milk<br>Boiled egg<br>Tea |
| *MORNING SNACK* | Milk or hot chocolate |
| *LUNCH* | Grilled fish with creamed spinach<br>Mashed potatoes<br>Ripe pear |
| *AFTERNOON SNACK* | Milk, cheese and biscuits |
| *DINNER* | Vegetable purée<br>Ham sandwiches<br>Tinned peaches |
| *EVENING SNACK* | Hot chocolate<br>Cottage cheese on toast |

# For slimmers

**BUFFET LUNCH**  Raw pickled rainbow trout or
Grilled herring

Roast Veal with herb sauce or
Sliced Turkey, ham or tongue

Boiled potatoes, baked onions
Mixed vegetables, soya beans in tomato sauce
A salad of tossed greens and vegetables

Cottage cheese with fruit
Fruit salad

# Practice

*Exercise I*  1  What do you notice about the food suggested for diabetics?

2  What is special about the food suggested for ulcer sufferers?

3  How is the menu for slimmers different from a normal menu?

*Exercise II*  Practise the conversation between a waiter in a restaurant and a guest who needs a special diet.

*Exercise III*  Plan alternative menus for people on a slimming diet.

# Useful phrases

We offer special menus for different diets.
We cater for various religious.
We guarantee the meat is pure beef.
We have a selection of vegetarian dishes.

# Chapter 11
# *SPECIAL FUNCTIONS*

## Catering for a banquet

Banqueting is a term used to cover special functions such as dinner parties, weddings, conferences, press gatherings, etc. In large first-class establishments they would take place in the various banqueting suites under the supervision and control of the Banqueting Manager.

The various types of functions come under three main headings:

*1. Social*
Weddings
Christenings
Private parties

*2. Public relations*
Press gatherings
Fashion shows
Exhibitions
Launching new products

*3. Seminars and*
   *Conferences*
Professional meetings
for those in industry
education etc.

The first contact between the Banqueting Manager and the client should be the signal for a file to be opened recording all the details concerning the function. The Banqueting Manager should suggest alternative menus with a 'cost per head' as well as layouts for different numbers of guests.

At the first meeting, after the booking has been confirmed, the following points should be checked:

1 Type of function
2 Date
3 Time
4 Number of covers
5 Price per head
6 Menu and method of service
(table service/self-service/buffet service)
7 Wines: inclusive or charged
8 Suggested table plan
9 Method of payment

When these details have been agreed, the following points should also be discussed:

1 Dancing, band, cabaret
2 Toastmaster/Master of Ceremonies
3 Place cards
4 Seating plan
5 Printing and layout of the menu
6 Special requirements

# Practice

**Exercise I** Study the information above and answer these questions:

1 What is a banquet?
2 What is one of the first things a Banqueting Manager should do once he has agreed to cater for the function?
3 What do you think are the disadvantages and advantages of table service and self-service?
4 What do you think 'place cards' are for?
5 What different table plans can you think of and what are the advantages of each?

**Exercise II** Without referring to the book, try and remember the fifteen points you would need to determine if you were organizing a banquet.

Tuomo Sipilä, Banqueting Manager at the *Runeberg* Hotel Restaurant is sitting in his office when the telephone rings:

| | |
|---|---|
| *Tuomo* | Good afternoon. Tuomo Sipilä, Banqueting Manager *Runeberg* Hotel Restaurant. Can I help you? |
| *James* | James Richardson, International Consultants Ltd. I'm phoning to enquire if you could cater for a dinner party we're planning to hold on 2nd of February. |
| *Tuomo* | In about a month's time. Yes, I think we can manage that. How many was it for? |
| *James* | There will be about twenty all told. We're setting up a Finnish subsidiary and we thought we might celebrate. |
| *Tuomo* | Certainly, sir. At what time had you planned to meet? |
| *James* | Oh around 7.30 would suit us fine and we had thought of your *Runeberg* Suite. There's rather an attractive picture in your brochure. |
| *Tuome* | Yes, the *Runeberg* suite will be free then. I'll send you a couple of menus with some suggested wines in my letter confirming this booking and we can discuss any further details at a later stage. |
| *James* | That sounds fine. I look forward to your letter and suggestions. The address is 12 Gloucester Avenue, London NW1 7EG. My phone number, by the way is 01 267 2290 |
| *Tuomo* | Thank you very much, Mr Richardson and you'll be hearing from us shortly. |

Here is the letter of confirmation Tuomo Sipilä wrote:

---

Mr James Richardson                    4 January 1981
INTERNATIONAL CONSULTANTS LTD
12 Gloucester Avenue
LONDON NW1 7EG

Dear Mr Richardson

I refer to your telephone call of 3 January 1981 and would like
to confirm the reservation of our Runeberg Suite for your
Dinner Party on Wednesday, 2 February 1981 at 7.30 pm for
approximately 20 guests.

I am enclosing two menus for your consideration. Menu 1 at
70 FIM and Menu 2 at 80 FIM are exclusive of a service charge
of 14%.

Drinks are charged at our standard prices according to the
quantities consumed. The final bill will be sent to International Consultants Ltd as requested.

We look forward to your instructions and will do our best to
make your dinner party a success.

                              Yours sincerely

                              *Tuomo Sipilä*

                              Tuomo Sipilä
                              Banqueting Manager
                              RUNEBERG HOTEL RESTAURANT

---

Here are the two menus he suggested:-

| MENU I (FIM 70) | MENU II (FIM 80) |
|---|---|
| Slightly salted salmon with mustard sauce | Crayfish soup |
| Fillet of veal with creamed morels | Wild duck with green salad |
| Mocha parfait | Melon stuffed with fresh raspberries |
| Coffee | Coffee |
| WINES | WINES |
| Bouchard, Beaune du Chateau | Amontillado |
| Chateau Servan La Tour, 1972 | Chateau Groleau–Côtes de Bourg 1974 |
| Monopol Madeira Rich Old Sweet | White Port |

Mr James Richardson phones through to Tuomo Sipilä to discuss some further points:

| | |
|---|---|
| *James* | Thank you, Mr Sipilä, for the two menus you sent us. They were both excellent, but we decided to take the second one as it seemed to us to be more Finnish. |
| *Tuomo* | Very good, sir. At 80 marks it is a little more expensive, but as you say it has more of a Finnish flavour. Now the table arrangements; do you want one large table? |
| *James* | No, we thought small individual tables for four would be suitable. As it's table service we feel this arrangement would be more intimate. By the way, we shall need brandy with the coffee. |
| *Tuomo* | That can easily be arranged. We stock most of the well-known brands. That presents no problem as the drinks are not included in the prices we quoted. |
| *James* | Quite. Well, I don't think we need to meet. I can leave all the arrangements in your capable hands. |
| *Tuomo* | Thank you again, sir, and we look forward to seeing your party on 2 February. Goodbye. |

# *Practice*

*Exercise I*  Study the conversations and the letter and answer the following questions:

1  What is the purpose of Mr Richardson's planned banquet?

2  What costs will be in addition to the food costs?

3  What sort of table and seating arrangements would Mr Richardson like to have for the banquet?

4  How will payment be arranged?

5  How did Mr Richardson hear about the *Runeberg Hotel*?

*Exercise II*  Refer back to the fifteen points you would need to determine when organizing a banquet and check the information you have for Mr Richardson's banquet against them. Is there anything that has been forgotten?

# Catering for a 3 day seminar

Mr Keith Adams, Congress Organizer, is checking through the arrangements for a three-day, post-conference seminar to be held at the Hotel *Neptune* with the Assistant Manager, Mr Jussi Korhonen.

**Keith**    I know that you have already received our outline programme, but I would just like to check the meal times to begin with.

**Jussi**    Well, breakfast will be served in the main dining room from 7 till 10 as usual. Do you have any special requirements there?

**Keith**    We do have rather a lot of Americans and Englishmen attending the seminar, so I think it would be a good idea to lay on some bacon and eggs, in addition to the normal fare

**Jussi**    Very good, sir. Lunch is at 12.30. Do you want to have the buffet lunch on Monday and Tuesday?

**Keith**    No, I don't think so. That would be boring. Can we have the normal waiter service on Tuesday? Something fairly light, fish or an omelette.

**Jussi**    And how about the afternoon coffee? Would you like that served in the lecture room?

**Keith**    No, I feel we could have a change of scene for that. Is the *Marine* Suite free? It has that wonderful balcony and the view down to the lake.

**Jussi**    Yes, I'm sure we can arrange that. Now, I gather that dinner on Tuesday will be later than usual because you are all going to sauna.

**Keith**    That is quite correct. Oh, by the way, I forgot to mention that we would like beer and soft drinks served in the changing rooms after sauna.

**Jussi**    Very good. Now do you have any special wishes as regards the food?

**Keith**    Well, we do have four vegetarians, that I do know and there are two participants from the Middle East so of course pork and shrimps will be out for them.

**Jussi**    I'll make a note of that. We have already received your suggested menu for the final farewell dinner on Wednesday evening.

*Keith*    Now to accompany the meal. I think that an Italian or Spanish red wine would be admirable. How about Chianti Ruffino?

*Jussi*    Very good sir. Are the table arrangements in order? You wanted seating arrangement 'A' on Monday and Tuesday and 'B' on Wednesday.

*Keith*    The only thing is that we are having some presentations during the dinner and I was wondering if we could have the table setting the other way round with the main table here at the top with the alcove behind.

*Jussi*    I think that can be arranged, sir. Now we haven't discussed table decorations yet.

*Keith*    I think that it would be appropriate to have the flags of the participating countries on the table and some flowers, perhaps pink carnations would be a neutral colour.

*Jussi*    Will you be requiring any background music at all?

*Keith*    I think not. It would be difficult to find something to suit all tastes. Incidentally, remember that we also have a welcoming cocktail on Monday evening, sherry for that and the usual fresh orange juice.

*Jussi*    I understand you have an excursion to the medieval castle on Wednesday. Will you be requiring packed lunches for that? One can get quite peckish after a long boat trip.

*Keith*    An excellent idea. But the participants will have to pay for that themselves. Oh, and talking of money, could you send the bill to the Congress Department of the Finland Travel Bureau Ltd, they are handling all the financial arrangements for the Congress. Well, I think that has covered all the points, hasn't it?

# *Practice*

***Exercise I***  Study the conversation between Keith and Jussi. Most of the basic arrangements have already been made but the extra details are very important. Using the check list below to help you, make notes of these details. The first has been done for you:

Breakfast requirements  *7-10 Main dining room English and Continental*

Lunch requirements:

Monday

Tuesday

Wednesday

Afternoon coffee

Cocktail reception

Tuesday dinner

Service to the sauna

Special diets

Wine

Table plans

Table decorations

Background music

Final billing

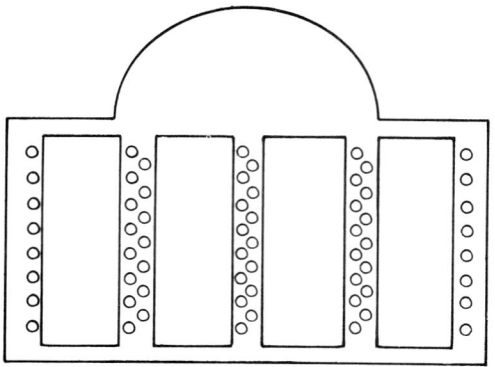 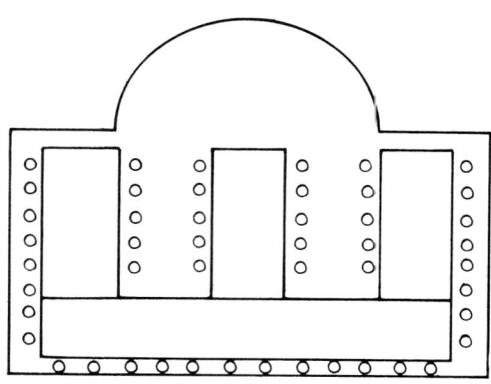

Table plans:   PLAN 'A'    PLAN 'B'

These were the original plans. How will Jussi change them to suit Keith's request?

**Exercise II**    Complete the following sentences with suitable words or phrases:

1    We can _____ for up to 50 people at one sitting.

2    We are pleased to _____ your reservation.

3    The drinks will be charged for according to the quantity _____.

4    I am _____ some sample menus for you to choose from.

5    Your company will be _____ in due course.

**Exercise III**    Plan a banquet or the meal arrangements for the participants attending a conference. Work in pairs or groups representing the client and the catering or restaurant manager. Your preparation should include the initial letters and as many of the finer details as possible.

# Useful phrases

What type of function is it to be?

How many people are to be catered for?

What type of service would you require?

What sort of table plan did you have in mind?

Do you have any special requirements?

When is the function to be held?

I'll send you some sample menus.

We shall confirm the booking by letter.

You will be hearing from us shortly.

The cost of the drinks will be charged separately.

That can easily be arranged.

Will there be any special dietary requirements?

# Chapter 12
# *CHEERS!*

## The barman in action

It will also be useful to know something about taking orders for drinks at the bar. Here are some orders:

| | |
|---|---|
| *Spencer* | A pint of bitter, please, barman. |
| *Barman* | I'm sorry, sir, but we only have two types of beer. The medium-strength beer and the export beer. |
| *Spencer* | Which is better? |
| *Barman* | Well, the export beer is stronger, but both are the light lager type. They are bottled, I'm afraid not draught. |
| *Spencer* | I'll have a bottle of the stronger one, please. |
| *Barman* | Certainly, sir, here you are. |

| | |
|---|---|
| *James* | A large scotch please. |
| *Barman* | On the rocks, sir? |
| *James* | No thanks. Just a little water please. |
| *Barman* | Anything else, sir? |
| *James* | Yes. A dry Martini with ice and lemon and something non-alcoholic for me please. I'm driving. |
| *Barman* | A tonic, fruit juice or a ginger ale perhaps? |
| *James* | Tomato juice please. Do you have any bits to nibble? |
| *Barman* | Certainly sir. I'll bring you over some crisps and peanuts. |

| | |
|---|---|
| *Wilson* | Two halves of bitter please. |
| *Barman* | Special or best? |
| *Wilson* | Oh, best please. |
| *Barman* | Anything else, sir? |
| *Wilson* | Yes. A vodka tonic please and do you sell cigarettes? |
| *Barman* | There is a machine over there sir. |
| *Wilson* | OK. Can you give me the right coins in the change please? |

# Practice

Using the expressions in the conversations above and the following list of drinks to help you, practice giving and taking bar orders in pairs:

**Spirits**
Vodka
Gin
Brandy/cognac
Whisky (Scotch/Irish/
Bourbon)
Rum

**Liqueurs**
Bénédictine
Chartreuse
Cointreau
Crème de Menthe
Drambuie
Grand Marnier

**Beers**
Bitter
Mild
Lager
Stout

**Aperitifs/fortified wines**
Sherry     Vermouth
Port     Pastis
Madeira

**Wines**
Bordeaux (claret)
           French red
Burgundy
White
Rosé
Champagne

**Non-alcoholic drinks**
Fruit juices
Tonic water
Soda water
Mineral water
Ginger ale

# *Useful phrases*

Draught or bottled?

On the rocks

Ice and lemon?

The cigarettes are in the machine.

Would you like to order wine with your meal?

We only serve wine by the bottle or by the glass.

The house wine is served in carafes and half carafes.

Medium, sweet or dry?

Last orders please!

Time gentlemen, please!

# Chapter 13
# *POLITE PHRASES*

*When your guests arrive, you should greet them according to the time of day:*

Good morning, sir.                      Good afternoon, madam.
Good evening.

*If you know your guest well:*

Good morning, sir. How are you today?
Good evening madam. It's nice to see you here again.

*If your guest asks you 'How are you?' you should reply:*

Very well thank you.

*When they leave:*

Goodbye, sir.
Goodbye madam, and we look forward to seeing you again.

*If you know the guest well:*

Bye bye, sir.

*Please and thank you*

Goodbye, sir, and thank you for coming.
We enjoyed the meal very much.—Thank you, madam, I hope you'll come again.

### You should use 'please' if you want something:

That's (£28) altogether, please.

### If you wish to give something that has not been asked for, don't say 'please', but mention what it is:

Here's your bill, sir.
Here's your pineapple juice, madam.
The soup, sir.

### If you are giving something that has been asked for:

Could I have some salt, please?—Certainly, sir. Here you are.
I'd like to see the menu.—Here you are, madam.

### Use 'please' when you wish to tell people politely what to do:

Would you come this way, please?
Please pay at the cash desk over there.
Please help yourself at the buffet table, madam.

## Affirmatives

### In English, just to say 'Yes' often doesn't sound very polite.

Here are some suitable phrases:
We'll be having dinner at 7.30 tonight.—Very good sir, I'll make a note of that.
Can we dress informally?—Certainly madam. That will be quite all right.
Do you take traveller's cheques?—Yes, of course. sir.

### To a customer you know well:

We'd like our usual table please–Right you are, sir.

## *Negatives*

### *And just saying 'No' is often impolite. Phrases are:*

Could we have a table for seven?—I'm afraid we're fully booked just now, sir.

I'm sorry, but we are closed on Mondays.

Is there a floorshow tonight?—No, as a matter of fact, there's no entertainment on Tuesday evenings, madam.

Do you have oysters on the menu?—Well, actually, we don't have oysters tonight, sir, but the crayfish are very good.

## *Apologies*

### *Polite negatives are often needed when apologizing:*

Excuse me sir, but I'm afraid we'll have to move you to another table. This one's already reserved.

I'm sorry madam, but I'm sure you'll understand.

### *If you didn't understand what a guest said, you can say:*

I'm sorry sir, but I didn't quite catch what you said.

### *Sometimes guests may apologize to you. You should answer:*

I'm sorry, we're a bit late for dinner I'm afraid.—Oh, that's perfectly all right, sir.

I hope we're not causing you a lot of bother.—No, not at all, madam.

You will find much more phrases in Chapter 9.

### Being helpful

Good morning. Can I help you?

I'll call you back as soon as I can (On the phone)
Yes sir, I'll make a note of that.
One moment, madam, I'll just check.
We'll attend to it right away. madam.

### Recommending

*Sometimes guests can't make up their minds. A gentle suggestion may help:*

I suggest you try the oxtail soup, madam.
I can thoroughly recommend the roast lamb, sir.

### Or mention alternatives:

You can either have the set lunch, or the *a la carte,* madam.

### Asking for information

*And finally, don't be afraid to ask your guests questions if they seem hesitant. In English, silence is not polite.*

What would you like to drink, madam?
And how about a sweet?
What name was it please?
Which would you prefer, sir, the dessert of the cheese board?
Is everything to your satisfaction, sir?

# *Practice*

*Exercise I*    What would you say in the following situations?

1. A regular customer arrives at your restaurant.
2. Your guests say goodbye to you as they leave.
3. You wish to know which guest is having soup.
4. A guest wishes to book a table for dinner but your restaurant is closed that evening for dinner.
5. You lead the way to a guest's table.

*Exercise II*    Give suitable responses to the following comments from guests:

1. Excuse me. Could you get me an ashtray?
2. I'm sorry to be such a nuisance but could I change tables?
3. I really cannot decide whether to have the lamb or the fish. What do you recommend?
4. We had a lovely meal. Thank you very much.
5. Can I see a wine list please?

*Exercise III*    Express the following in a more polite way:

1. The bill you have to pay is £50.
2. Any problems?
3. Which do you want, red wine or white?
4. You don't pay me, you pay at the till.
5. You can't sit there, it's reserved.

*Exercise IV*    Practise responding politely to different situations in pairs.

# Chapter 14
# *EVERYONE TO HIS OWN TASTE*

## British food and eating habits

Honesty and simplicity are the great strengths of cooking in the British Isles. While cooks in other countries rely on garlic and spices to enliven their food, the British approach lets the ingredients speak for themselves. Holiday-makers returning from abroad have popularized many foreign dishes in Britain. But anyone who has had a superb English meal, for instance, oysters, followed by a roast saddle of lamb, and a Stilton cheese with a glass of port, can testify to the glories of British cooking. Above all, those traditional pillars of English cuisine, breakfast and high tea, are unsurpassed anywhere in the world.

## *Breakfast*

Anyone arriving from abroad and staying at a good English country hotel, might still rub his eyes in disbelief at the breakfast table. After a choice of cereals or fruit juices, there is a choice of fried eggs, ham and eggs, bacon and eggs, scrambled eggs with sausages and grilled tomatoes, fried kidneys or smoked fish such as the famed kipper and the smoked haddock. In addition there is often porridge, oatmeal cooked in water and traditionally eaten with salt, sometimes covered with plenty of fresh cream, or stewed fruits, such as prunes, apricots or apples. Afterwards, you can have buttered toast with orange marmalade, jam or honey. To go with it all is the ever-present enormous pot of tea.

# The inventive
# American cuisine

The United States is a vast pantry. On American grasslands that are as large as some of the countries of the world, roam enormous herds of beef cattle. An overflowing abundance of fruit and vegetables of countless varieties springs from its earth. A profusion of lobsters, crabs, clams, oysters, shrimps and fish is drawn from its waters. Its golden waves of grain reach to endless horizons.

If America is a pantry, the American kitchen is a laboratory. It is equipped with a wealth of culinary machines and gadgets designed to simplify the task of preparing the products of nature's generosity for the dinner-table. America's obsession with labour-saving tools and mechanical devices was translated, first, into such simple gadgets as apple peelers and hand-cranked ice-cream freezers, and later into space-age ovens, high-speed blenders, electric juicers and an extensive catalogue of other implements that have transformed the process of cooking.

Ironically, this amalgam of abundance and mechanics has not resulted in a fancy American cruisine. Generally, American cooking is unsophisticated and straightforward, concerned with content rather than form.

The best-known and most popular American foods are grilled steaks, hamburgers, fried chicken, boiled lobster and fried fish. All of these dishes can be delicious, and none requires much cooking flair. Some recipes for Southern fried chicken, however, are jealously guarded family secrets, and a pure beef hamburger with onions and relish on a fresh sesame-seed roll can taste good enough to be a product of culinary magic.

The simplicity of most cooking in the United States is deceptive. Although the American cook may not spend long hours over a hot stove, and, due to a highly efficient food distribution system, big-city cooking tends to be the same across the country, the variety of regional foods in America is formidable. New England cooking has little in common with Pennsylvania Dutch cooking. Neither has a Montana rodeo roast with a magnificent traditional Hawaiian *luau*. Indian influences in the Southwest, and French-Spanish influences in Louisiana are still apparent. But the settlers from England, Holland and a dozen other countries as well, who tamed the Atlantic coast and gradually pushed the frontier back across the continent to the Pacific Ocean, had little time or inclination for ceremony or ritual in cooking.

The first problem was survival. The settlers held that if the ingredients were good and properly cooked, whether fried, baked or boiled, that's all that could, or should, be desired.

RE - G

Over the decades, this no-nonsense approach to cooking sank deep into the American culture, although even on the frontier a woman could gain fame for the lightness of her corn biscuits or the delicacy of her hot berry pie. Gradually, however, regional distinctions began to emerge and flourish so that, for example, there is now fried Kentucky ham with red-eye gravy, smoked Pennsylavia Dutch ham with dried apples, cornmeal-coated Texas ham, thinly sliced Virginia ham with hot biscuits, Missouri baked glazed ham. Similarly, clam chowder was given a milk base in New England, a tomato base in the mid-America region, and the clams in the chowder were sometimes replaced by oysters in the South.

Aside from regional differences, there were lessons learnt from later arrivals from Europe who brought with them to America a taste and a skill for a different kind of kitchen craft, for sauerbraten in Milwaukee, for Polish sausage in Chicago and for a dozen different spaghetti sauces in New York.

There is a versatility and ingenuity to the American cuisine which belies its basic simplicity. It is as varied, inventive and ultimately indefinable as America itself.

# Practice

*Exercise I*   1   Why is the USA compared to a pantry?

2   What is an American kitchen like?

3   Mention some well-known American dishes.

4   Why is big-city cooking very much the same all over the United States?

5   Where does the no-nonsense American attitude to cuisine come from?

*Exercise II*   According to the text, which of the following statements about American food are true and which are false?

1   American foodstuff is plentiful and diverse mainly because it is produced in a great variety of physical environments.

2   Many different gadgets were invented in the USA to make preparation easier and quicker.

3   As a result, American cooking is very specialized and complicated.

4   American food is basically very simple and is more or less the same in all parts of the country.

5   It is because of the arrival of later immigrants from Europe that American cooking is now so difficult to define.

*Exercise III*   What is your opinion of American cooking?

# Around Europe

**AUSTRIA**  Soups are generally substantial particularly when served with dumplings such as *leberknödelsuppe* (liver dumplings in beef broth). The most popular meats are veal (Wiener Schnitzel) and pork which is often served roasted. There are various varieties of sausages usually flavoured with garlic. Austria is world famous for its confectionery, cakes, flans and tarts like *apfelstrudel* and chocolate *sachertorte* which are often very rich and served with cream.

**BELGIUM**  Cafés serve rich and satisfying soups with sandwiches. A great deal of meat is eaten especially beefsteak, pork and veal. Beer is often used in cooking, for example in *carbonnades flamandes* which is collar of beef and onions braised in beer. A typical dish is *waterzooi*, a chicken and vegetable stew served with boiled potatoes. Chicory is a popular vegetable and is often served as a main dish, or eaten raw in a salad. Typical seafood includes mussels, shrimps and especially eels. Pickled eels fried in oil and served cold with jelly are a delight.

**CZECHOSLOVAKIA**  A square meal offered to the foreign visitor starts off with assorted cold meats, famous Prague ham, smoked tongue, Russian crab meat in mayonnaise, eggs with caviar, all garnished with plenty of pickles. Roast pork, duck and goose as well as meat with a thick gravy are often accompanied by the beloved *knedliky* dumplings and *zeli,* spiced red cabbage.

**DENMARK**  The great speciality is the *smorrebrod,* an open sandwich of endless variety usually based on rye bread, with such ingredients as herring; fried eel, ham and shrimps. These are followed by hot dishes including fried fish, especially plaice, served with a sauce or rissoles. Danish pastries are very varied and there is a famous dessert called *rodgrod med flode,* jelly of redcurrants and other fruits served with cream.

**FRANCE**  One of the main features of French cooking is the use of alcohol, mostly wine, but also brandy and in Normandy, cider or Calvados. In the south you will find numerous versions of the famous *bouillabaisse* (fish stew) and in the south-east *cassoulet,* a stew of haricot beans and either pork or goose. The Burgundy area has produced *boeuf à la Bourguignonne* (beef cooked in red wine) and many dishes from the Dordogne area contain truffles. There are nearly 300 different cheeses from the soft ones like *Brie* and *Camembert* to the veined *Bleu d'Auvergne* or *Roquefort* (made from ewe's milk).

**GERMANY**  There are numerous regional specialities and dishes tend to be heavy and well-spiced. Pork dishes are popular and there are many varieties of sausage, *wurst,* often served with shredded pickled cabbage, sauerkraut. Soups are very filling and often contain dumplings. Fish dishes are based on trout, carp and salmon. Game dishes are superb. There are many kinds of cream-filled cakes and pastries and heavy sweets of marzipan or cheese cakes.

**GREECE**  Generally speaking the cuisine is Continental. Popular soups include *psarosoupa,* a fish and vegetable soup and *kotosoupa,* chicken broth with egg and lemon. Local specialities include *moussaka,* minced meat, aubergine and spices; *keftedhes,* fried meat balls; *arni souvla,* lamb on a spit and the famous *dolmadhes,* vine or cabbage leaves stuffed with minced meat and rice. *Kolokythia,* baby marrows, called courgettes in France and zucchini in Italy, are a popular vegetable.

**HUNGARY**  One of the few original cuisines in Europe. Paprika dishes come in a great variety. The six basic dishes are *gulyás,* a soup with cubed beef and diced potatoes spiced with sweet red paprika; *pörkölt* pork, veal, beef or chicken stew; *paprikás,* a meat fricassée sprinkled with sour cream; *tokány,* a beef stew with black pepper flavouring; *rostélyos,* stewed sirloin cutlet in paprika sauce and finally *halászlé,* Hungary's fish soup answer to bouillabaisse. *Rétes,* a flaky pastry comes filled with cherries, apple, nuts, almonds, poppy-seed or cottage cheese.

93

ITALY   Many popular dishes are based on pasta in a variety of forms—macaroni, rice (base for risotto) and spaghetti. There are a number of vegetable soups including minestrone and a good choice of antipasti (hors d'oeuvres). *Ossobuco* (veal knucklebone in a thick sauce) is excellent. *Zabaglione* (egg yolks, Marsala and sugar) is popular for dessert as too are the wealth of *gelati* (ice-cream).

LUXEMBOURG   The country enjoys a good reputation for its cuisine. Among the national dishes are: *Treipen* (Black Pudding) and sausages with horseradish; smoked pork and broad beans; jellied suckling pig; calf's liver quenelles (forcemeat) and delicious Ardennes ham, served raw or cooked. Trout and pike are excellent and during the shooting season jugged hare is a favourite.

NETHERLANDS   Breakfast usually consist of thinly sliced Dutch cheese, prepared meat and sausage served with several varieties of bread. A typical lunch is *koffietafel,* bread, various cold meats, cheeses and conserves served with a side dish, either omelette or salad. Some of the national dishes include *erwtensoep,* rich pea soup and *boerenkool met rookwoorst,* curly cabbage with smoked sausage. *Rijsstafel* is a dish which reflects its Indonesian origin by including boiled rice, chicken, shrimps, small red fish and fried fruit. Cheeses are varied and include *Gouda* and *Edam.*

NORWAY   Lunch consists of *smorbrod* (open sandwiches) or *koldtbord* (ample cold buffet), famous for its variety of dishes including smoked salmon, fresh lobster and shrimps. Some specialities are *fiskeboller* (fish rissoles) *gravlaks* (fish pudding and salmon). Game including ptarmigan and *dyrestek* (reindeer) are in season at certain times of the year.

POLAND   *Barszcz,* a beetroot soup served in large helpings along with sausage, cabbage, potatoes, sour cream and *czarny chleb* (coarse rye bread) is a favourite. *Chlodnik* is a cold rich cream soup with crayfish. It is worth trying *flaki,* a dish of tripe served boiled or fried and *bigos,* sauerkraut with smoked meats. Hare cooked in cream, roast venison and smoked ham or pork loin are regular meat dishes.

**PORTUGAL**  There is a wealth of sea food available. Many are based on *bacalhau* (cod), fresh or salted, tunny, mackerel, sardines and *lagosta* (crayfish). *Gaspacho* is an iced soup of bread, tomatoes, onions garlic, cucumber and pimentos. Of the meats, pork is best. It can be roast or grilled and it features in some fish dishes, for example, *Consoada,* baked cod with peas, fried pork and fritters. Creme caramel and rice pudding with cinnamon are popular. Crystallized fruits and sugar plums are worth trying.

**SOVIET UNION**  *Zakuski* are salted spicy hors d'oeuvres. The caviar is justly world-famous. It comes from two major sources: salmon from the Far Eastern rivers supply the red caviar and black caviar is supplied by the sturgeon family, that from the white Beluga sturgeon is considered the best. Siberian *pilmeny* in a ravioli-like combination of meat and dough. *Borsch* and *bliny* (leavened pancakes) taste best with sour cream. Of Georgian food, *shashlik,* lumps of spiced mutton skewered on a dagger, is justly famous.

**SPAIN**  Much of the cooking is done in olive oil and rice figures in many of the national dishes such as *paella* (rice with chicken, fish and vegetables). *Tortillas* (omelettes) are also popular. Stews are varied and include *Fabada,* haricot beans, bacon and sausage. One of the best known sweets is *turrón de almendras,* made of almonds, egg whites and sugar. There is a variety of cheeses from the soft *getilla* to the smoked *asturias* and *manchego* made from ewe's milk.

**SWEDEN**  *Smögasbord,* a kind of extensive hors d'oeuvre of pickled or smoked herring, liver pâté, sausage, smoked salmon, sliced meats, salads and cheeses. Popular dishes also include meatballs, several varieties of sausage and *kaldolmar* (minced meat and rice baked in cabbage leaves). Also crayfish, lobster and many kinds of game such as venison and moose meat.

**SWITZERLAND**   The most famous dish of Swiss origin is *fondue* (melted cheese with white wine and kirsch added, into which bread is dipped). Pork and veal form the basis of most meat dishes and trout, perch and pike, fresh from the mountain steams and lakes are very good. *Gruyère* and *Emmenthal* are probably the best-known cheeses.

**YUGOSLAVIA**   Yugoslav cuisine incorporates features of both European and Oriental cookery. Tea is served with lemon or rum. Coffee is normally black. Among meat dishes as *cevap,* large pieces of highly spiced pork; *podvarak,* various kinds of meat with sliced sour cabbage and *kapama,* braised lamb always served with spinach. *Halva* pastry stuffed with chopped walnuts and honey is also a well-known sweetmeat.

# Practice

*Exercise I*    According to the descriptions of food given for each country, match the specialities on the left with the countries on the right.

| | | | |
|---|---|---|---|
| 1 | Seafood sandwiches | A | Hungary |
| 2 | Paprika dishes | B | Greece |
| 3 | Pork dishes | C | Soviet Union |
| 4 | Cheese fondue | D | Italy |
| 5 | Bliny | E | Portugal |
| 6 | Pasta dishes | F | Austria |
| 7 | Bouillabaisse | G | Spain |
| 8 | Pastries and tarts | H | Denmark |
| 9 | Stuffed vine leaves | I | France |
| 10 | Omelettes | J | Switzerland |

*Exercise II*    From your own knowledge of dishes from different parts of Europe, what do you think of the descriptions of food given for each country? Do you agree with everything? Have you any additional comments to make?

# Useful phrases

A choice of cereals or fruit juices

A selection of pies and cakes

Plain cooking

Fancy cooking

The recipe is a closely guarded secret

Flavoured with (garlic)

Served with (cream)

Garnished with (mushrooms)

Many varieties of (sausage)

97

# Chapter 15
# *THE WORLD OF*
# *THE CHEF*

This book is intended to help you with the English you will need outside the kitchen. Inside the kitchen is a different world of language. It might be useful, however, to include a few culinary terms and names for you to refer to.

## Some raw materials

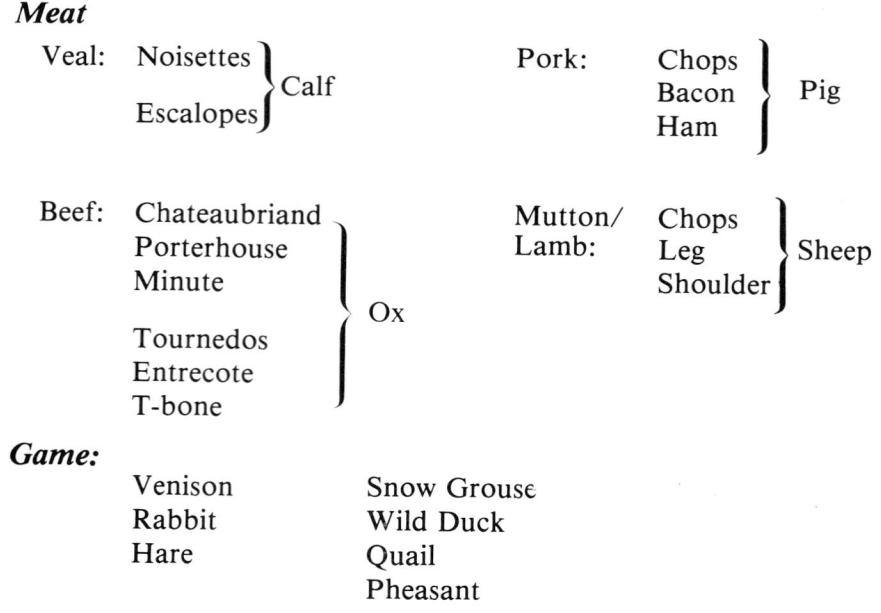

*Meat*

Veal: Noisettes
Escalopes ⎫ Calf

Pork: Chops
Bacon ⎫ Pig
Ham

Beef: Chateaubriand
Porterhouse
Minute
Tournedos ⎫ Ox
Entrecote
T-bone

Mutton/
Lamb: Chops
Leg ⎫ Sheep
Shoulder

*Game:*

Venison
Rabbit
Hare

Snow Grouse
Wild Duck
Quail
Pheasant

### Fish

Salmon
Trout
Pike
Perch
Pike-perch
Bream
Cod
Plaice
Sole
Kipper
Haddock
Herring

### Poultry

| Chicken: | Leg |
| --- | --- |
| | Breast |
| | Wing |

Goose
Duck
Turkey

### Shellfish/Molluscs

Prawn/shrimp
Oyster
Crab
Squid
Snail
Mussel
Lobster

### Vegetables

| | |
| --- | --- |
| Asparagus | Served boiled on their own with a sauce, in salads or as a soup. |
| Beans | Broad beans   Usually served boiled.<br>French beans   Boiled or sliced and fried in butter or oil. |
| Beetroot | Usually served raw in salads. |
| Cabbage | Can be boiled or creamed, used in soups, or served raw in salads |
| Carrots | Boiled or creamed, used in soups, purées and stews. You can also grate raw carrots and serve them as a salad. |
| Cauliflower | Boiled, creamed, or gratinated. |
| Celery | Often served raw. |
| Cucumber | Often served raw in salads. |
| Leeks | Served boiled, gratinated or used in soups. |
| Lettuce | Used for salads and garnishing. |
| Onions | Used in flavouring and to season different kinds of dishes. Can be served fried, pickled or as a soup. |
| Peas | Boiled, or used in soups. |

| Potatoes | Can be served in the following ways: |
|---|---|
| | French fried potatoes/Chips (Br.) |
| | Fried potatoes |
| | Boiled potatoes |
| | Mashed potatoes |
| | Baked potatoes |
| | Duchess potatoes |
| Radishes | Usually served in salads. |
| Spinach | Boiled or creamed. |
| Sprouts | Boiled or creamed. |
| Sweet peppers | Used in salads, as garnishes, in casseroles or stuffed. |
| Tomatoes | Served raw in salads or as garnishes, in soups and sauces, or sometimes stuffed. |

## *Fruit and Berries*

| | | |
|---|---|---|
| Strawberries | Raspberries | Blueberries |
| Gooseberries | Cranberries | Blackberries |
| Cherries | Apples | Oranges |
| Lemons | Grapefruits | Pears |
| Bananas | Peaches | Pineapples |
| Grapes | Melons | Apricots |

## *Cheeses*

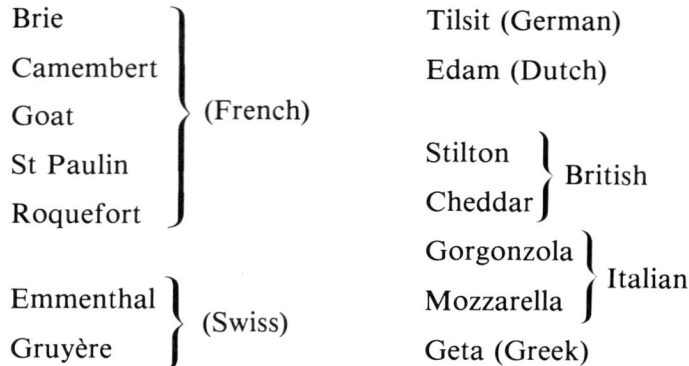

Brie  
Camembert  
Goat  
St Paulin  
Roquefort  
} (French)

Emmenthal  
Gruyère  
} (Swiss)

Tilsit (German)  
Edam (Dutch)

Stilton  
Cheddar  
} British

Gorgonzola  
Mozzarella  
} Italian

Geta (Greek)

# Notes on some famous French cheeses

## *What to ask for*

**BRIE**  A large creamy cheese with a soft white rind. The correct description of this type of cheese is 'soft paste'. Originally from the Ile-de-France, a whole Brie measures about 14″ across, but it's generally sold in smaller portions which are packed in wedge-shaped boxes.

**CAMEMBERT**  Camembert traditionally comes from Normandy. Like Brie, it has a rich creamy texture and a soft white rind. But being about 4″ across, it matures quicker, and has a stronger, full-bodied taste. Half sizes and individual portions are available.

**GOAT CHEESES**  These are very popular in France and are made all over the country. The best known include Banon, (wrapped in chestnut leaves): Valençay: Sainte Maure: and Chabichou.

**ST. PAULIN**  St. Paulin is a semi-hard cheese which is easily recognised by its washed, bright orange rind. The cheese itself is yellow and mild, with a smooth texture. Port Salut was the monastery where the cheese was originally made and this famous variety is still an excellent choice.

**ROQUEFORT**  Superb blue cheese with a reputation for being the most expensive in the world. Made from ewe's milk, Roquefort comes only from Aquitaine. The caves in which it ripens have the unique properties which give the cheese its strong, rich taste.

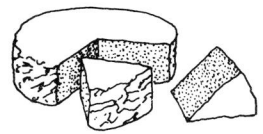

# *How to choose it*

**BRIE**  Open the box in the shop and press your fingers gently on the wrapped cheese. It should be springy to the touch. The box should always be packed tight with cheese. If the cheese has shrunk, that means it's stale.

**CAMEMBERT**  Follow the same instructions as for Brie. Always remember that when you're buying any of these soft paste cheeses, it's best to get them a little at a time so they're always in peak condition when you serve them.

**GOAT CHEESES**  Some goat cheeses have a white flowery rind like Brie, others have a washed rind like St. Paulin. The consistency of the cheeses is just as variable, so choose them the same way you would any other cheese. Goat cheeses are generally small and are invariably fairly strong.

**ST. PAULIN**  A whole St. Paulin weighs about 5lb so smaller portions are available. Why not try the small round versions packed in red or yellow wax to keep the cheese fresh. You'll find there's a subtle difference in the flavour.

**ROQUEFORT**  A whole Roquefort is very large. Individual requirements can be cut to order or bought in pre-packed portions. Check that the cheese is very white, the blue veins are evenly distributed and the texture is smooth and firm—almost like butter. Although Roquefort has a distinctive smell, it should not be overpowering.

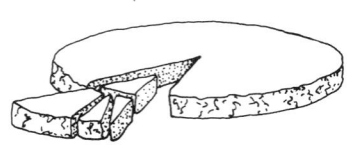

# How to eat it

**BRIE**  Depends entirely on your taste, but most people like it when it's rich and creamy. At this stage you can even eat the rind. If you prefer Brie when it's stronger and a bit runny, wait till the rind turns a mottled brown. Then eat the cheese, but not the rind.

**CAMEMBERT**  The same principles that apply to a Brie also apply to a Camembert i.e. it's a matter of personal taste. Don't let anyone tell you a Camembert should only be eaten when it's strong and runny, if you like mild and creamy!

**GOAT CHEESES**  Like most others, goat cheeses are usually eaten at the end of the meal when they can be enjoyed with any good wine—red, white or rosé. A glass of full-bodied beer goes extremely well with a fresh goat cheese.

**ST. PAULIN**  St. Paulin is a good cheese to eat and a good cheese to cook with. As it's French, why not do as the French do and eat it after the main course and before desert for a change. Any light wine goes with it perfectly.

**ROQUEFORT**  Generally, Roquefort is eaten at the end of a meal and it should be accompanied by an equally superb wine such as a Châteauneuf-du-Pape. Roquefort can also be used to make a splendid blue dressing for salads or add class to cânapés.

# *How to store it*

**BRIE** If it's not ripe enough when you buy it, keep it somewhere warm for a while. But if it's just right, put it in the bottom of the fridge until an hour before the meal. Any left-overs should be re-wrapped and put back in the box. Kept properly, the cheese will ripen from the outside towards the centre.

**CAMEMBERT** Treat it the same way as Brie. If any Camembert is left at the end of a meal, put it back in the box and store it cut-side up in the bottom of the fridge. This will keep the cheese well inside the rind.

**GOAT CHEESES** Keep them in a cool place after you've wrapped them carefully to prevent the air getting to the cheese.

**ST. PAULIN** Like other semi-hard cheeses, St. Paulin should be stored in a suitably cool place. Always wrap the cheese carefully, so that no air can get to it. And take it out an hour before you eat it. Follow this rule for all cheeses.

**ROQUEFORT** A cheese which is said to have been Charlemagne's favourite, must be stored properly if you are going to do it justice. Ideally, it should be wrapped and then stored in a plastic container to keep it moist and fresh, either in the bottom of the fridge or some other suitably cool place.

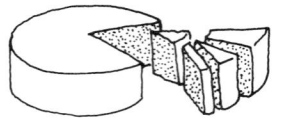

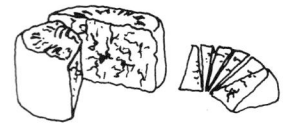

# Methods of preparation

**BAKE**  To cook in an oven. e.g. potatoes, cakes, bread.

**BASTE**  To moisten the product with its own juices, fat or sauce.

**BEAT**  To mix vigorously. e.g. eggs.

**BOIL**  To cook in water or other liquid at 100°C.

**BRAISE**  To brown meat or vegetables in fat, then to cook slowly in a small amount of liquid.

**BROIL**  The American equivalent of 'to grill'.

**CREAM**  To mix sugar, shortening and other ingredients until smooth.

**CREAMED**  To cook by braising something with cream. e.g. creamed mushrooms

**CRUMB**  To coat with breadcrumbs before frying.

**DEEP FRY**  To cover in hot fat which is deep enough to cover the item.

**DICE**  To cut into small cubes.

**FLAMBER (French)**  To pour alcohol on a food item and light it. e.g. crêpes flambées

**FRY**  To cook in fat in a frying pan.

**GARNISH**  To decorate food for presentation at the table. e.g. fish garnished with slices of lemon.

**GRATE**  To rub foods against a grater. e.g. grated carrots, cheese etc.

**GRATINATE**  To brown the top of a sauced item. e.g. cauliflower au gratin.

| | |
|---|---|
| **GRILL** | To cook under direct heat. e.g. grilled liver |
| **MARINATE** | To soak in marinade, a spiced liquid mixture of oil, wine, vinegar and herbs to make tender. e.g. marinated herring |
| **PEEL** | To remove the skin from fruit or vegetables. e.g. peeled almonds. |
| **PLANK** | To broil meat or fish on a special wooden board e.g. planked beefsteak |
| **POACH** | To cook under boiling point in a hot liquid. e.g. poached eggs |
| **ROAST** | To cook fish or meat in an oven. e.g. roast beef |
| **SALT** | To add salt to an item of food |
| **SAUTÉE** | To cook very slowly in a small amount of fat. e.g. sautéed mushrooms |
| **SEASON** | To add spices, sauces or other ingredients to improve the taste. |
| **SHRED** | To cut into thin pieces. e.g. shredded cabbage |
| **SIMMER** | To cook in liquid just below boiling point |
| **SLICE** | To carve into slices. |
| **SMOKE** | To cook fish, meat etc in smoke e.g. smoked whitefish |
| **SOAK** | To keep in a liquid for a long time. |
| **SPICE** | To add spices such as salt and pepper. |
| **STEAM** | To cook in steam formed by boiling water. e.g. steamed haddock. |
| **STEW** | To simmer in a liquid until tender. e.g. stewed meat, prunes. |
| **WHIP** | To beat rapidly. e.g. whipped cream. |

# *Practice*

***Exercise I***    Answer these questions as simply as possible:

1    What are baked potatoes?
2    What is braised beef?
3    What is deep-fried squid?
4    What are sautée potatoes?
5    What is smoked haddock?

***Exercise II***    From the list of raw materials and methods of preparation, make up some dishes to complete menus of your own.